A SELF HELP BOOK FOR MENTAL HEALTH AFTER ADDICTION

CRAFTED BY SKRIUWER

Copyright © 2024 by Skriuwer.

All rights reserved. No part of this book may be used or reproduced in any form whatsoever without written permission except in the case of brief quotations in critical articles or reviews.

For more information, contact : **kontakt@skriuwer.com** (www.skriuwer.com)

TABLE OF CONTENTS

CHAPTER 1: UNDERSTANDING LIFE AFTER ADDICTION

- You learn what to expect and why emotions and thoughts can feel intense.*
- Physical, emotional, and relationship changes are explored.*
- Tips to spot triggers and keep watch for relapse signs.*

CHAPTER 2: FIRST STEPS TO EMOTIONAL STABILITY

- Techniques to calm strong feelings early on.*
- Building routines for steady morning and evening habits.*
- Handling sudden urges with simple exercises and clear communication.*

CHAPTER 3: BUILDING A STRONG MINDSET

- Automatic thoughts and core beliefs explained.*
- Turning negative self-talk into balanced, helpful statements.*
- Methods to set small goals and find daily motivation.*

CHAPTER 4: MANAGING WORRY AND RESTLESSNESS

- Recognizing triggers for anxiety or impatience.*
- Quick fixes like breathing exercises and mindful distractions.*
- Advanced methods like "grounding" and creating structured routines.*

CHAPTER 5: STRENGTHENING CONNECTIONS WITH OTHERS

- Why healthy bonds matter for long-term stability.*
- Communication tips for honest, respectful relationships.*
- Boundaries, trust rebuilding, and finding supportive groups.*

CHAPTER 6: PLANNING A SAFE FUTURE

- Setting realistic goals for work, home, and personal growth.*
- Managing finances and safeguarding your environment.*
- Creating backup plans for high-stress times or unexpected events.*

CHAPTER 7: TRANSFORMING HARMFUL THOUGHTS

- Identifying negative loops and self-critical beliefs.*
- Step-by-step methods to replace distorted thinking with balanced views.*
- Practical tools like journaling and labeling emotions accurately.*

CHAPTER 8: USEFUL ACTIVITIES FOR THE MIND & BODY

- Simple daily routines for physical activity and mental clarity.*
- Creative outlets, mini-workouts, and safe social distractions.*
- Ideas to stay motivated and reduce boredom or restlessness.*

CHAPTER 9: HANDLING URGES AND CRAVINGS

- Early signs of cravings and how to respond quickly.*
- Specific techniques—urge surfing, emergency plans, and distraction.*
- Recognizing triggers that spark old harmful behaviors.*

CHAPTER 10: BUILDING SELF-WORTH WITHOUT HARMFUL HABITS

- Moving past guilt and shame, separating actions from identity.*
- Daily acts of self-care and healthy boundaries to respect yourself.*
- Setting realistic goals to confirm your sense of personal value.*

CHAPTER 11: COMMUNICATING IN A NEW WAY

- Active listening and "I" statements to reduce conflict.*
- Clear expression of feelings and needs to build trust.*
- Handling criticism or heated moments calmly, without aggression.*

CHAPTER 12: PROBLEM-SOLVING METHODS FOR EVERYDAY LIFE

- Structured approaches to break down big and small problems.*
- Balancing logical steps with emotional handling.*
- Brainstorming, prioritizing, and adjusting plans when setbacks occur.*

CHAPTER 13: BALANCING WORK, HOME, & FREE TIME

- Identifying all your roles—worker, parent, friend, etc.—and finding harmony.*
- Practical strategies like time-blocking, delegation, and shared calendars.*
- Scheduling leisure and breaks to prevent burnout.*

CHAPTER 14: FINDING MEANING IN THE MIDDLE OF UNCERTAINTY

- Defining personal values and noticing small sources of fulfillment.*
- Managing fear of the unknown and using reflective practices.*
- Turning setbacks into lessons and finding higher purpose in daily acts.*

CHAPTER 15: HANDLING ANGER AND FRUSTRATION

- Early signs of anger and ways to cool down fast.*
- Assertive communication instead of outbursts or hidden resentment.*
- Healthy outlets like art, exercise, or open dialogue to release tension.*

CHAPTER 16: SUPPORT SYSTEMS AND POSITIVE ROLE MODELS

- How different types of support—friends, professionals, groups—work.*
- Finding trustworthy people who respect your boundaries and encourage growth.*
- Role models, mentors, and ways to pick the right influences for you.*

CHAPTER 17: DEALING WITH DISAPPOINTMENT AND SETBACKS

- Why setbacks happen and how to respond without panicking.*
- Separating an event from your self-worth to avoid unnecessary guilt.*
- Turning disappointment into insight and updating goals accordingly.*

CHAPTER 18: KEEPING A HEALTHY BODY AND MIND OVER TIME

- Daily habits—sleep, food choices, light exercise, regular checkups.*
- Stress-management routines and creating a calm living environment.*
- Handling relapses in self-care and maintaining motivation over the long term.*

CHAPTER 19: TRUST, HOPE, AND HEALTHY PLANS

- Rebuilding self-trust and mending relationships through consistent actions.*
- Recognizing genuine hope versus ignoring real challenges.*
- Creating future plans that respect your limits and stay adaptable.*

CHAPTER 20: MOVING FORWARD WITH INNER STRENGTH

- Summarizing all tools—emotional regulation, problem-solving, self-care.*
- Staying vigilant against relapse while embracing growth.*
- Viewing life as an ongoing journey of learning and discovery, free from old harmful habits.*

CHAPTER 1: UNDERSTANDING LIFE AFTER ADDICTION

Introduction
Life can take a big turn after you stop certain harmful habits. This chapter will show you what it means to go through day-to-day life once an addiction is behind you. There might be confusion about what to do next or how to handle memories of your old life. You may feel unsafe in some moments or wonder if you made the right choice. However, understanding what happens inside you and around you can help you feel calmer and more sure of yourself.

Below, we will look at deeper information to make sense of life after addiction. We will use simple language to help you see the path more clearly. You will learn about possible changes in your emotions, thinking, and physical health. We will also look at some advanced tips that can help you see patterns in your thoughts and guide you toward better choices.

1.1 Shifts in Thoughts and Feelings

Once you have stopped using harmful substances or engaging in addictive behavior, you might notice that your feelings seem sharper or more intense. This could happen because the substance or behavior you depended on was dulling your senses. Now that it is not present, your brain might react more strongly to everyday life.

- **Thought Changes**: Thoughts may race or slow down. Your mind might jump to worries, regrets, or guilt. Sometimes you might find yourself looking back and feeling upset about what you did in the past. You might also notice new hopes or goals forming in your mind. Understanding that these changes are common can give you comfort and help you manage them without panic.
- **Emotional Changes**: Emotions might swing from anger to sadness or from relief to fear. These strong shifts often happen because your brain and body are readjusting. The highs and lows can be tiring, but they are also normal. Recognizing these swings can prepare you for them. You can practice calm breathing, simple grounding exercises, or quick relaxation methods during strong emotional surges.

1.2 Physical Adjustments

There can be physical symptoms as well. You might feel new levels of tiredness, headaches, or body aches in the early stages of recovery. This may happen because the body is healing from the effects of the substance, or from long periods of stress tied to addictive behavior. Each day, your physical state can vary, but there are methods to help your body adjust:

- **Proper Rest**: Setting a bedtime and keeping a steady sleep schedule can help the body heal. Good rest can support emotional balance too.
- **Nutritious Eating**: When you feed your body in a healthy way, it helps with healing. You might try including more vegetables, fruits, and protein, as well as drinking enough water.
- **Safe Movement**: Light exercises, like walking or gentle stretching, can help the body release stress. They can also improve your mood by raising the level of feel-good chemicals in the brain.

1.3 Changes in Relationships

When addiction is active, relationships often suffer. After you stop the harmful behavior, you may find that people around you act in new ways. Some might be happy to see your progress, while others might be cautious or worried that you could slip back into old habits. Here are a few things to keep in mind:

- **Trust Issues**: If you hurt or lied to friends and family during your addiction, they may need time to trust you again. Try to stay patient and open to honest communication.
- **New Expectations**: People might expect you to act differently right away. This can feel like a lot of pressure. Remember that change often happens in steps, and it is normal to have ups and downs.
- **Meeting People in Supportive Groups**: You might find that talking with others who have gone through similar experiences makes you feel less alone. Sharing stories in a safe space can help you gain strength and new ideas.

1.4 New Freedoms and Challenges

Ending addiction can bring a sense of freedom. You may notice you have more time or money or feel lighter now that you are not tied to something harmful. But, along with these positive changes come challenges:

- **Free Time**: You might feel uneasy when you have more free time. It can be risky if you do not plan activities. Finding useful things to do can reduce boredom or loneliness, which are big triggers for relapse.
- **Pressure to Fill the Gap**: The addictive behavior used to be a big part of your day. Now there is an empty space. You might feel tempted to fill it with a new unhealthy habit if you are not careful. Learning safe ways to spend time, like reading simple articles, doing crafts, or talking with supportive friends, can help.
- **Handling Sudden Triggers**: Old triggers can pop up out of nowhere. A certain smell, place, or event can make you think of using again. Part of your new life is to learn how to spot triggers and decide on a good way to handle them.

1.5 Approaches to Understand Your Path More Clearly

Your mind might need extra attention now. Here are some advanced ideas that can help you gain a clearer view:

1. **Track Your Mood and Thoughts**: Writing down what you think or feel each day can help you see patterns. You might notice that certain times, places, or people lead you to feel low or high. By seeing these patterns, you can prepare solutions beforehand.
2. **Healthy Habit Creation**: Rather than relying on motivation alone, set up easy routines. For example, every morning, take five minutes to do slow breathing. Every evening, write down three things that went well. Small tasks can build a stable daily rhythm.
3. **Low-Intensity Mind Focus Exercises**: If you feel scattered, try a simple moment of focus. Sit in a chair, close your eyes for one minute, and notice your breathing. If your thoughts wander, gently bring them back to your breath. This can help you handle stress and sharpen your focus over time.
4. **Practical Worries vs. Unhelpful Worries**: Sometimes you worry about things you can solve (like paying a bill). Sometimes you worry about things you cannot control (like what others think about you). Learning to separate the two can help you direct your energy where it can actually make a difference.

1.6 Seeing Yourself Clearly

Your self-image might shift a lot. You may feel proud of quitting addiction, but you could also feel shame or regret about past actions. Understanding how to see yourself fairly takes time. Here are steps you can try:

- **Self-Check**: Once a week, write a short note to yourself about what you did well and what you want to improve. This way, you track your progress without being too harsh on yourself.
- **Allow Your Feelings**: Anger or sadness might show up. Let yourself feel them safely, and remember that these feelings do not define you. They come and go.
- **Positive Self-Instruction**: Use encouraging words when you talk to yourself. For example, say "I am learning new things each day" instead of "I always mess up." These small word choices can have a big impact on your mindset.

1.7 Guarding Your Progress

One key part of staying well after addiction is looking out for warning signs of relapse. It does not help to worry constantly, but being aware can protect you. Some signs include:

- **Feeling Overconfident**: Believing you are "cured" might lead you to put yourself in risky situations.
- **Slipping Back into Old Routines**: Going back to the places or people who influenced your harmful behavior can make it more likely that you will return to it.
- **Ignoring Emotions**: If you keep painful feelings bottled up, they can build until you look for relief in the old habit.

Keeping track of how you feel and being honest with yourself are key to staying safe. If you notice warning signs, talk to someone you trust, like a friend, family member, counselor, or support group member.

1.8 Key Points from Chapter 1

1. You might feel more sensitive or emotional once you stop a harmful habit.

2. Physical symptoms are common, and taking care of your body can help you adjust.
3. Relationships may need time to heal. Communication and honesty can help.
4. You have more freedom now, but it requires careful planning to stay safe.
5. Simple and advanced self-awareness methods can keep you informed about your emotions and triggers.
6. Building a more positive self-view involves noticing negative thoughts and trying to replace them with fair ones.
7. Keep watch for relapse signs, but do not live in fear. Awareness can keep you on track.

Conclusion

Life after addiction can bring both challenges and new chances. This chapter gave you a basic look at what to expect and how to face it without feeling lost. You learned about changes in your thoughts, body, and relationships, and how to handle the freedom and risks that come with a new way of living.

The next chapter will take you from understanding life after addiction to practical steps for emotional stability. You will explore how to stay balanced when feelings and thoughts get intense. Always remember: knowledge about what is happening in your mind and body can help you move forward day by day in a safer and healthier way.

CHAPTER 2: FIRST STEPS TO EMOTIONAL STABILITY

Introduction
Emotions can feel like wild waves. One day you may feel confident, and the next day you may feel overwhelmed by sadness or anger. After quitting an addictive habit, these mood shifts can be even stronger. The goal of this chapter is to show you how to handle these emotions in a balanced way without feeling trapped. You will read about practical methods, from daily habits to advanced techniques, that can help you get a more stable hold on your feelings.

2.1 Why Emotions Seem More Intense

When you were stuck in harmful behavior, substances or compulsive actions often masked or dulled your feelings. Now, without that mask, it can feel like you are being hit with an overload of emotion. Your body and mind must re-learn how to handle stress, sadness, or fear without the old "solution." This can feel uncomfortable, but it is part of the healing process.

- **Sudden Feeling Swings**: You might have trouble predicting your mood. Something small could irritate you much more than expected, or you could feel weepy for no clear reason.
- **Relearning Self-Control**: Part of emotional stability is understanding when you need to calm yourself down, and when it is healthy to let the feelings out. You are not just quitting a habit; you are building a new skill set of self-regulation.

2.2 Basic Methods for Emotional Control

Here are some reliable methods you can practice every day to help reduce emotional chaos:

1. **Controlled Breathing**: Take slow breaths through your nose, hold for a moment, then breathe out gently through your mouth. Doing this for just a few minutes can lower stress levels and help you think more clearly.
2. **Body Awareness**: Pay attention to places in your body that feel tense. Maybe your shoulders are raised, or your hands are clenched. Relax that area on purpose. This helps shift your focus away from racing thoughts.

3. **Simple Self-Reminders**: Tell yourself a short phrase like, "I will be okay," or, "This feeling will pass." Repeating this can keep anxious or angry thoughts from spiraling.

2.3 Establishing a Morning and Evening Routine

Consistency can help keep your moods in check. When your body knows what to expect each day, it might feel safer.

- **Morning Routine**: Set a specific time to wake up. Do a short breathing exercise, have a glass of water, and eat a basic breakfast. Even a simple plan can create a sense of order in your day.
- **Evening Routine**: Pick a bedtime. Before sleeping, dim the lights and avoid using devices that shine bright lights in your eyes. If you are uneasy, write down your worries on a piece of paper. This can ease the mind before rest.

2.4 Developing a Support System

When dealing with emotional upsets, having people you can talk to is very helpful. Support can come from many sources:

- **Family and Friends**: Choose those who care about you and do not judge you harshly. Ask if you can call them when you feel bad or have a question.
- **Support Meetings**: You might join local or online groups made for people who have quit harmful habits. Listen to their stories and share your own if you feel ready.
- **Professional Help**: A counselor or therapist can give you advanced tools to manage anger, sadness, or fear. They can also help you spot deeper issues that might lead to emotional swings.

2.5 Learning to Say "No"

Many people in recovery find it hard to say "no," either to old friends offering substances or to new requests that add stress to their lives. This can overload your mind and lead to strong feelings of frustration or panic. Here are some methods for saying "no" firmly:

- **Set Clear Boundaries**: Let people know kindly that you are not able to do certain things, such as going to bars or parties, or lending money for risky uses.
- **Practice Short Scripts**: Come up with a few short answers you can use in tough moments. For instance, "I'm working on keeping my mind safe, so I have to skip that event." This saves you from the pressure of coming up with something on the spot.
- **Self-Care Afterward**: Even if you say "no," you might still feel uneasy. Treat yourself to some calming activity afterward, like taking a warm bath or reading something uplifting.

2.6 Simple Exercises for Emotional Balance

Here are a few straightforward techniques to help handle strong feelings:

1. **Five-Sense Check**: When you feel overwhelmed, pause and list five things you see around you, four things you can touch, three things you can hear, two things you can smell, and one thing you can taste. This method brings your attention to the present moment, reducing the power of negative thoughts.
2. **Mini-Meditation**: Close your eyes, take a deep breath, and focus on a calming thought such as a calm location. Spend one minute with that thought. When you open your eyes, you might feel slightly more at ease.
3. **Tense and Release**: Tighten the muscles in your hands or feet for a few seconds, then let them relax. Move on to other parts of your body. This helps you learn the feeling of relaxation by comparison.

2.7 Recognizing Personal Triggers

Certain situations or people might stir up painful memories or push you toward harmful actions. Identifying these triggers can help you plan ahead:

- **People**: Maybe a friend you used to use substances with can trigger a craving. Or a family member who made you feel upset might trigger anger.
- **Places**: A neighborhood bar or a certain street might bring back memories of when you felt out of control.
- **Feelings**: Stress, sorrow, or low self-esteem can also act as triggers, pushing you to look for comfort in old, harmful ways.

Make a list of triggers you can think of. Next to each trigger, write down a plan. For example, if you pass by a certain street on your way to work, maybe you can take another route. If you must see a person who upsets you, plan to keep the visit short and have an exit plan in case you feel stressed.

2.8 Advanced Techniques for Emotional Understanding

Sometimes basic methods are not enough. Here are some more advanced ideas:

1. **Emotion Name-Tagging**: When a strong feeling appears, label it: "This is anger," "This is sadness," "This is fear." Labeling helps your brain separate the feeling from who you are. It is a mental note that says, "I am experiencing this emotion, but it is not my entire identity."
2. **Mindful Thought Checking**: If a thought like, "I am worthless," pops up, test if it is accurate. Is there a real reason you are worthless? Likely not. This kind of checking can reduce the power of negative thoughts.
3. **Stepping Back**: If you notice a pattern, such as feeling down every Monday morning, you can prepare helpful steps for those days. Maybe schedule a short chat with a friend or plan something positive on Mondays. This does not solve every problem, but it can smooth out rough patches.

2.9 Using Positive Activities as Outlets

Emotions, especially negative ones, build up if we do not handle them. Instead of keeping them inside, look for safe ways to express them:

- **Art or Writing**: Drawing, coloring, or writing poems can let you show complex feelings. You do not need to be "good" at it; the aim is to let the emotion flow.
- **Music**: Listening to calming music or playing an instrument can shift your mood.
- **Physical Activity**: Activities like a gentle walk, light home exercise, or simple sports can help your body release tension. Your brain might also produce chemicals that improve your mood.

2.10 Adjusting to Unexpected Emotions

Even when you are doing your best, sudden or heavy emotions can appear. Here are a few pointers on what to do:

- **Accept the Feeling**: It is normal to feel sad, angry, or anxious now and then. Telling yourself it is okay to feel this way reduces the sense of shame or panic about having the emotion.
- **Find a Quick Outlet**: If sadness hits, let yourself cry for a short while. If anger arrives, write about it in a journal or talk to a trusted person. Getting the feeling out in a safe way can keep it from turning into harmful behavior.
- **Use Soothing Tools**: Breathing exercises, a warm drink, or even a comforting object (like a stress ball) can help lower the intensity of the feeling.

2.11 Handling Emotions with Others

Sometimes we want to share our feelings with someone, but we do not know how. Here are some tips:

- **Pick the Right Person**: Choose someone who will listen without harsh judgment.
- **Use Clear Words**: Say something like, "I feel really tense and I need to talk." This is more helpful than hinting or hoping they will guess how you feel.
- **Be Open to Feedback**: Sometimes the person may suggest solutions. Other times they might just listen. Let them know what you need: do you just want someone to hear you out, or do you also want advice?

2.12 Dealing with Relapse Worries

When you feel overwhelmed, you might worry about relapse. Here are some strategies to keep that worry from controlling you:

- **Have a Plan**: Know what to do if you start having strong cravings or negative thoughts. Maybe have a list of numbers to call or places you can go.

- **Replace the Thought**: If a thought like, "Using again will help me feel better," appears, try substituting it with, "Using again will cause me more problems." This might feel forced at first, but repeated practice can make it stronger.
- **Seek Guidance Quickly**: If you feel close to a relapse, do not wait. Call a supportive friend or reach out to a counselor. Early intervention can stop a small problem from becoming a bigger one.

2.13 Reviewing Daily Success

A helpful approach to staying emotionally stable is to reflect on what went well each day. This is not about ignoring problems but about giving yourself time to see the positives:

1. **End-of-Day Reflection**: Write down one or two good things that happened. They can be very simple, like "I had a nice phone call with a friend," or "I stuck to my plan and did not return to an old routine."
2. **Check Your Feelings**: Write down which emotions you noticed the most that day. If you spot a pattern of stress around certain tasks or people, that is a clue to make changes.
3. **Positive Closing**: Before bed, say a short statement to yourself. For example, "I am thankful for getting through this day in a healthier way." This helps your mind end the day with a sense of accomplishment.

2.14 Key Points from Chapter 2

1. Emotional intensity is normal after addiction because substances or harmful actions used to dull feelings.
2. Basic coping methods, like controlled breathing and routines, can lower stress.
3. Support systems, whether friends, family, or groups, help you handle tough emotions.
4. Learning to say "no" and setting limits can prevent emotional overload.
5. Simple exercises, such as the Five-Sense Check, can bring you back to reality when you feel overwhelmed.
6. Tracking personal triggers will help you plan ways to manage them.
7. Advanced methods like emotion labeling and thought checking can give you more control over negative thinking.

8. Finding positive outlets for emotions, such as art or music, reduces the chance of relapse.
9. Unexpected emotions can happen, but having a quick, safe outlet can stop them from growing.
10. Talking about emotions with the right people can bring comfort and practical advice.
11. Having a plan for relapse worries can keep you from feeling trapped by fear.
12. Reviewing your day and noticing small successes can slowly build your confidence over time.

Conclusion
This chapter outlined the first steps you can take to steady your emotions after addiction. By using regular routines, basic calming methods, and advanced tools for self-understanding, you can keep your emotional health on a more even track. Remember: strong feelings are part of being human, especially in recovery. You are not alone in this. Support is available, and many helpful tools exist.

In the next chapter, you will learn how to build a strong mindset to protect your mental well-being. Combining what you learned here about emotional control with a firm sense of purpose and self-belief will allow you to keep moving forward in a safer way.

CHAPTER 3: BUILDING A STRONG MINDSET

Introduction

Once you have begun to manage your emotions and keep them in check, the next step is to develop a solid mindset that supports long-term progress. A strong mindset is not just about thinking positive thoughts. It also involves being prepared for problems, having a clear view of who you are, and learning how to stay focused on the path you want to follow. This chapter will show you how to fortify your thinking patterns in a way that helps you move past old hurdles and protect your recovery.

We will talk about how your thoughts shape the way you see your life. We will look at how to handle negative self-talk and how to build a supportive inner voice. You will also learn some advanced concepts on motivation and self-guidance that you might not hear in basic self-help advice.

3.1 Understanding the Power of Thoughts

Your thoughts can either help you or drag you down. Sometimes, certain beliefs can limit what you think you can do. By understanding the power of these internal messages, you can begin to gain control over how you respond to life events.

- **Automatic Thoughts**: These pop up instantly in response to a situation. For example, if you drop a glass, you might immediately think, "I always mess up." These kinds of quick thoughts can color how you feel about yourself.
- **Core Beliefs**: These are deeper ideas that shape your view of the world. For instance, if you believe that you are incapable of handling stress, you may remain stuck in fear whenever a tough problem appears.

Your goal is to become aware of these patterns, so you can rewrite them in a way that is accurate and helpful.

3.2 Differences Between a Weak Mindset and a Strong Mindset

It helps to see what a weaker mindset might look like. This does not mean you are bad if you notice these traits in yourself. Instead, it is a sign of what you can improve:

- **Weak Mindset Signs**:
    1. Constant excuses for not trying new things.
    2. Blaming others or outside events for every problem.
    3. Avoiding changes because of fear of failure.
    4. Giving up easily when tasks become difficult.

A stronger mindset, on the other hand, does not mean you never make mistakes or never feel upset. It means you face life with more honesty, willingness to learn, and steady resolve:

- **Strong Mindset Signs**:
    1. Willingness to put in the effort, even if an outcome is not guaranteed.
    2. Taking responsibility for choices and actions.
    3. Seeing mistakes as chances to learn, instead of proof that you are unfit.
    4. Maintaining hope, even in challenging situations.

3.3 Steps to Build a Solid Inner Foundation

Here are some ways you can begin to shift your thinking and develop a stronger mindset:

1. **Observation Without Judgment**: Start by noticing your own thoughts. If you catch yourself thinking, "I cannot do this," label it as a thought, not a truth.
2. **Use Concrete Evidence**: Ask yourself if there is real proof for your negative thought. Often, negative thoughts are based on fear or habit, not facts.
3. **Slow Progress**: Making sudden, huge changes in mindset can be overwhelming. Instead, pick small goals, such as challenging one negative thought per day, and then build from there.

3.4 Strengthening the Mind Through Positive Action

While your thoughts play a big role, your actions also feed into your mindset. Here are some actions that can support a stronger outlook:

- **Setting Clear, Small Goals**: Rather than saying, "I want to be fully healthy," pick a smaller aim, like, "I will do fifteen minutes of safe exercise today." Achieving small goals can boost your confidence.
- **Rewarding Your Efforts**: Notice when you follow through on a plan. This does not have to be a big celebration; a simple mental note such as, "I did what I said I would do, and that's good," can strengthen your mind.
- **Challenging Yourself in Safe Ways**: Try something slightly outside your comfort zone, like learning a new skill or speaking up in a support meeting. Success in small challenges can build resilience.

3.5 Removing Old Self-Limiting Beliefs

Many people have old beliefs that keep them from moving forward. These might sound like, "I always fail," or, "No one will respect me." Such beliefs can form during childhood or from hurtful relationships or from failures in the past.

1. **Identifying the Belief**: Write down your repeated thoughts: "I'm not smart," "I can't handle stress," or "I'm always unlucky."
2. **Looking for Evidence**: Ask yourself, "Is there proof that this belief is always true?" Usually, you will find at least one example that contradicts it.
3. **Changing the Statement**: Replace the old belief with something more balanced. For example, if you think "I'm always unlucky," try a new statement like, "Bad things have happened in the past, but I can create better outcomes with careful steps."

3.6 Guarding Your Mind from Negative Influences

A strong mindset also requires careful protection. Negative influences can weaken your resolve, making you more prone to unhelpful thoughts. Here are ways to shield your mind:

- **Limit Negative Media**: Constant sad or fear-based news can make you feel hopeless. Give yourself permission to step away from media if it causes you too much stress.
- **Choose Uplifting Contacts**: Spend time (either in person or online) with people who aim to grow. They do not have to be perfect, but they should care about supporting each other in healthy ways.
- **Recognize Triggers**: If certain topics or discussions always upset you, try limiting those conversations. Be clear about your limits with those around you.

3.7 Strengthening Self-Talk

Self-talk is the voice inside your head that comments on everything you do. If it is negative, it can weaken your mindset. If it is balanced, it can help you push ahead:

- **Identify Your Inner Tone**: Is your self-talk usually harsh or critical? Do you call yourself names like "stupid" or "lazy"? These negative labels can become part of how you see yourself.
- **Practice Kind Language**: Instead of scolding yourself with, "I am such a failure," try saying, "I had a hard time with this, but I can look for a better way."
- **Use Neutral Phrases**: If positive phrases feel too forced, use neutral statements like, "I can try to handle this in a calm way."

3.8 Steady Motivation: Going Beyond Feelings

It is easy to take action when you feel motivated. The problem is that motivation can rise and fall. One day you might be full of energy, and the next day you might feel exhausted or unsure. Building a strong mindset means learning to continue healthy actions even when you do not feel like it.

- **Use Routines**: If you do something at the same time each day, you will rely less on mood. For example, if you decide that 8 a.m. is your time to do a short exercise, then do it regardless of how you feel that morning. Over time, this routine can become a natural part of your life.

- **Track Progress**: Keeping a small journal of daily achievements can remind you why you started in the first place. Reading past entries can spark a renewed sense of purpose.
- **External Motivators**: Talk about your goals with a friend or join a supportive forum. Knowing that someone else is expecting a progress update can push you to stay on track.

3.9 Handling Setbacks with a Strong Mindset

No matter how prepared you are, setbacks happen. You might miss a goal or slip into an old pattern for a day or two. A strong mindset does not ignore setbacks; it uses them as a chance to grow.

- **Step 1: Pause and Look at What Happened**: Did stress at work push you into old habits? Did an argument with someone distract you from your goals?
- **Step 2: Find the Lesson**: Maybe the lesson is that you need a better plan for dealing with stress, or you need to communicate your feelings earlier so they do not build up.
- **Step 3: Move Forward**: Once you know the lesson, decide on one action you can take right away to prevent the same slip. This can help you feel back in control quickly.

3.10 Using Your Imagination in a Helpful Way

Imagination often gets a bad name because we think it only applies to children or daydreams. In reality, it can be a strong tool for building a healthy mindset:

- **Helpful Visualization**: Spend a few minutes picturing yourself handling a tough situation with calm. For example, imagine having a difficult talk with someone, but staying level-headed. Then picture yourself finishing the talk feeling proud that you remained calm.
- **Remove Negative Scripts**: If you find yourself visualizing bad outcomes (like failing again or embarrassing yourself), try swapping that scene with a more balanced one. This does not mean ignoring real risks; it means reminding yourself that good outcomes are also possible.

3.11 Golden Insights for a Stronger Mind

Below are some less-common tips that can strengthen your mind beyond basic self-help:

1. **Create a "Mental Safe Spot"**: Pick a short phrase, or a simple object (like a small stone in your pocket) that you link with safety. Each time you feel anxious or negative, hold the object or repeat the phrase to bring your mind back to a place of calm.
2. **"If/Then" Plans**: Make mini-plans for potential problems. For example, "If I get too anxious in a group chat, then I will step away for five minutes and breathe." This structured plan can help you act instead of freeze in the moment.
3. **Switch Tasks When Stuck**: If you notice that you are stuck in a loop of negative thinking, switch to a simple physical task, such as folding laundry or cleaning a small area. Shifting your focus can break the loop and give your mind space to reset.

3.12 Building Mental Strength in Everyday Life

Some people think building a strong mindset only happens during big challenges. However, you can practice mental strength in normal, everyday moments:

- **Daily Decisions**: Small choices, like sticking to a set bedtime or preparing a simple, nutritious meal, strengthen your mind's resolve to do things that benefit you.
- **Social Interactions**: Practice clear communication. If you feel upset at a friend's comment, calmly explain how you feel. This might be difficult at first, but it will build confidence and self-respect.
- **Observation in Routine Tasks**: Even when washing dishes or sweeping floors, notice your thoughts. Are you complaining internally or feeling thankful that you can keep your space clean? These small mindset checks can add up.

3.13 Common Pitfalls to Avoid

In working on a stronger mindset, watch out for these traps:

1. **All-or-Nothing Thinking**: Telling yourself, "If I do not succeed perfectly, then I have failed entirely." This can cause you to give up too soon.
2. **Comparing with Others**: You might see people who seem to handle life without trouble. Remember, everyone has hidden struggles. Focus on your own growth instead.
3. **Allowing Negative Self-Talk to Repeat**: If you slip, do not spend days putting yourself down. Notice that you slipped, figure out why, and move forward.

3.14 Actionable Exercises

Try these exercises to make your mindset stronger in a more active way:

1. **Mindset Journal**: Each night, write a short summary of one challenge and how you responded. Did you think in a balanced way, or did you jump to harsh thoughts? Over time, you will see your own patterns.
2. **Positive Data Log**: Each time you handle a situation well, write it down. For example, "Today, I told my boss I needed more time for a task, and I did not feel guilty for asking." Keep these notes in a small notebook. On days you feel useless or stuck, read them to remind yourself of your abilities.
3. **Micro-Challenge**: Pick a tiny challenge each day and see it through. It can be something like solving a puzzle, making your bed as soon as you wake up, or learning a new word. Overcoming small obstacles can build a sense of self-trust.

3.15 Key Points from Chapter 3

1. Your mindset is shaped by automatic thoughts and deeper beliefs.
2. A strong mindset includes accountability, willingness to learn, and balanced self-talk.

3. Challenging negative beliefs with facts and logic can free you from old limitations.
4. Supporting actions, like keeping routines and taking on small goals, strengthen your mind.
5. Guarding your mind from negative influences helps you stay on track.
6. Self-talk plays a major role in how you see yourself and your ability to grow.
7. Motivation can go up and down, but a strong mindset helps you keep moving despite those shifts.
8. Recovery from setbacks is a learning process, not just an event.
9. Imagination and planned responses (like "If/Then" statements) can boost mental readiness.
10. Practice mental strength in everyday life, not just when problems appear.

Conclusion

Building a strong mindset is an active process that goes beyond simply "thinking positive." It involves noticing your thought habits, taking small steps to shift them, and practicing consistent behavior that supports your goals. Whether you are dealing with daily stress or facing bigger hurdles, the tips in this chapter can guide you to a more grounded way of thinking.

Next, in Chapter 4, we will look closely at how to manage worry and restlessness—common problems that can test even the strongest mindset. You will learn helpful techniques to keep these troubling feelings from taking over, so you can protect your progress and keep moving toward a healthier life.

CHAPTER 4: MANAGING WORRY AND RESTLESSNESS

Introduction
Worry and restlessness can feel like constant buzzing in your mind and body. They can make it hard to focus, mess up your sleep, and lead to poor choices if you seek short-term relief in unhealthy ways. After addiction, you might be more sensitive to these troubling states because the old habit used to serve as an escape. Now, you need fresh methods to handle worry and restlessness without returning to harmful behaviors.

In this chapter, we will discuss what worry and restlessness look like. We will also explore ways to calm the mind and body before anxiety spins out of control. You will learn practical tools you can apply immediately, as well as more advanced methods that can help you gain deeper control over these feelings.

4.1 Recognizing the Signs

Worry often starts as small thoughts, such as, "What if things go wrong tomorrow?" Restlessness can show up in physical ways: fidgeting, pacing, or feeling unable to sit still.

- **Mental Signs of Worry**: Thoughts loop around a problem, imagining worst-case outcomes, difficulty concentrating, or jumping from one concern to another.
- **Physical Signs of Restlessness**: Tense muscles, tapping feet, shifting in your seat, heart rate increasing, or mild trembling in the hands.

Catching these early signs lets you use quick fixes before worry and restlessness become overwhelming.

4.2 Common Triggers for Worry and Restlessness

Knowing what sets off these feelings helps you take action:

- **Uncertain Situations**: Not knowing what will happen at work or with family can cause the mind to run in circles.
- **Large Tasks**: Feeling like you have too many things to do can stir up a sense of panic.
- **Negative Self-Talk**: If you think you cannot handle problems or that you are weak, you might start worrying more than needed.
- **Over-Stimulation**: Crowds, loud noises, or too many online alerts can create inner tension.

Write down any triggers you notice. This helps you see patterns and plan ahead.

4.3 Quick Ways to Reduce Worry

When a wave of worry hits, these short methods can help bring some relief:

1. **Box Breathing**: Inhale for a count of four, hold your breath for four, exhale for four, and pause for four. Repeat several times. This helps reset your nervous system.
2. **Muscle Relaxation**: Clench your fists for a few seconds and release. Do the same with your shoulders, face, and legs. Let go of stored tension bit by bit.
3. **Check the Facts**: Ask yourself, "What do I know for sure, and what am I guessing?" Often, we spin worries out of guesses or fears rather than facts.

4.4 Using Physical Movement for Restlessness

If you feel physical tension or an urge to move without aim, safe exercise can be your friend:

- **Short Walk**: A five-minute walk outside (or even inside a corridor) can help burn off nervous energy.
- **Gentle Stretching**: Stretch your arms, legs, and back to relax stiff muscles. This also brings your focus to your body, giving your mind a break from spinning thoughts.

- **Light Household Chores**: Something as basic as washing dishes or folding laundry can channel restlessness into a productive action. Just be mindful not to slip into hectic rushing; aim for a calm, steady pace.

4.5 Thought Management for "What Ifs"

One of the main fuels for worry is the "What if?" question. "What if I lose my job?" "What if my cravings return?" The mind can create endless scary possibilities. Here is how to handle them:

1. **Write Them Down**: Putting your worries on paper can make them look more manageable.
2. **Plan or Let It Go**: If there is something you can do to prepare, do it. If not, remind yourself that worrying alone does not solve anything.
3. **Set a Worry Time**: Allow yourself 15 minutes at a certain part of the day to think about worries. When worries pop up outside that window, remind yourself they can wait. This trains your brain to stop fixating all day long.

4.6 Advanced Anxiety-Reducing Methods

Sometimes quick fixes are not enough. Below are more advanced methods for deeper relief:

1. **Calming Imagery**: Picture a calm place or a safe scene. Focus on small details like the colors or sounds you might find there. This can slow racing thoughts.
2. **Grounding Through the Senses**: Sit still and name three things you can see, two things you can hear, and one thing you can touch. This refocuses your attention on the present moment instead of on anxious thoughts.
3. **Adaptive Problem-Solving**: Break big problems into small steps. If you feel uneasy about finances, for example, pick one action: check your bank balance, then plan the next step based on what you learn.

4.7 Reducing Restlessness with Structure

Restlessness can increase when your life feels scattered or uncertain. Creating structure can help:

- **Daily Routine**: Wake up and go to sleep at the same time, if possible. Have a simple plan for meals and tasks. A steady routine can calm the mind by offering predictability.
- **Activity Blocks**: Group your tasks into blocks of time. For instance, from 9 to 10 a.m., you will focus on a specific job. Then, from 10 to 10:15 a.m., you take a break. This reduces aimless wandering.
- **Give Yourself Checkpoints**: Every couple of hours, pause and see if you are on track or if you need a break. This helps prevent pent-up restlessness from building throughout the day.

4.8 Healthy Distractions vs. Avoidance

When worry or restlessness become too heavy, it is useful to switch to a healthy distraction. However, there is a difference between helpful distractions and total avoidance:

- **Healthy Distraction**: Engaging in an activity that is safe, has a clear benefit, or teaches you something new—like reading an interesting article, writing in a journal, or doing a puzzle.
- **Avoidance**: Hiding from your problems by watching hours of mindless TV, sleeping all day, or ignoring important tasks. This can lead to more stress later.

Aim for short, helpful distractions that let your mind rest, but return to your tasks when you feel calmer.

4.9 Restlessness and the Urge to Relapse

Feeling restless can be a big trigger for old habits. Your mind might tell you that using again will calm the racing inside. Here are some strategies:

1. **Have a "Relapse Emergency Plan"**: Keep phone numbers of supportive people you can call. Remind yourself of the problems that come with going back to your old ways.
2. **Physical Release**: If the urge grows strong, try a more intense but still safe physical activity like brisk walking or a quick set of squats. Wear out the restless energy.
3. **Mental Reminder**: Keep a small note in your pocket or phone that lists the reasons you quit. Read it when you are tempted. This can bring your mind back to reality.

4.10 Sleep and Its Role in Cutting Worry

Poor sleep can increase anxiety and make restlessness worse. Improving your sleep schedule is a potent way to manage these feelings:

- **Set a Bedtime**: Pick a consistent bedtime, even on weekends. This trains your body's internal clock.
- **Wind-Down Time**: Spend 30 minutes before bed doing calm activities such as reading a light book, listening to soft music, or writing down your thoughts.
- **Limit Stimulants**: Avoid coffee, strong tea, or energy drinks late in the day. These can keep your body tense.

Getting adequate rest might not solve every problem, but it gives your brain the energy it needs to face challenges calmly.

4.11 Talking About Your Worries

Many people try to handle their worries alone. This can make them grow in silence. Consider speaking about your concerns:

- **Close Friend or Family Member**: Pick someone you trust who will not judge you harshly.
- **Support Groups or Online Communities**: Sharing your worries with people who understand your struggles can lessen the feeling that you are isolated.

- **Professional Help**: A counselor or therapist can teach you structured ways to manage chronic worry. They might suggest cognitive techniques or guide you in problem-solving tasks you have never tried before.

4.12 Mindfulness for Worry and Restlessness

Mindfulness is a practice of paying attention to the present moment without letting your thoughts roam into regret or fear about the future:

1. **Watch Your Breath**: Spend a few moments noticing the in-and-out rhythm. If your mind drifts, gently return your focus to the breath.
2. **Body Scan**: Mentally move through each part of your body from head to toe, noting how it feels. This can show you places you hold tension.
3. **Mindful Walking**: Walk slowly and notice how your feet meet the ground, how the air feels, and the sights around you.

The aim is not to block thoughts but to simply observe them without letting them spiral into bigger worries.

4.13 Golden Insights for Easing Restlessness and Worry

Here are some less common but powerful ideas:

1. **Mini-Focus Shifts**: When panic feelings rise, pick one object in the room and study it for a few seconds. Note its color, shape, and texture in your mind. This intense focus can momentarily break the chain of anxious thoughts.
2. **Scheduled Body Movements**: If you know you get restless every afternoon, plan a short break around that time. Do simple stretches or walk around the block. Catching restlessness early is easier than dealing with it once it grows.
3. **Talk to Yourself in Third Person**: Instead of saying, "I am so anxious," try, "(Your Name) is feeling anxious right now." This can create a small gap between you and the feeling, making it seem less overwhelming.

4.14 Handling Restlessness in Social Settings

Social events can be tense if you struggle with worry or an urge to move around:

- **Plan Your Approach**: If you feel overwhelmed at large gatherings, stay near someone you trust. Step outside for a breath of fresh air if you need a break.
- **Have a Time Limit**: Decide beforehand how long you will stay. This can stop you from feeling trapped.
- **Pick Conversation Topics**: If talking with new people makes you uneasy, think of simple subjects to bring up, such as shared interests or a kind observation about the setting.

4.15 Key Points from Chapter 4

1. Worry often begins in the mind, while restlessness often shows up in the body. Catching early signs helps you respond faster.
2. Triggers can include uncertain situations, big tasks, negative self-talk, or busy environments.
3. Quick fixes like box breathing or muscle relaxation are useful in preventing worry from spiraling.
4. Structured routines and daily plans can reduce restlessness.
5. "What If?" thoughts feed anxiety; writing worries down and taking action (if possible) can limit their power.
6. Use healthy distractions wisely, and avoid total avoidance.
7. Have a relapse emergency plan if restlessness tempts you to go back to old habits.
8. Good sleep is a big factor in lowering worry and restlessness.
9. Talking to a friend, support group, or professional can ease anxious thoughts.
10. Mindfulness practices can ground you in the present, preventing runaway thoughts.
11. Less common tricks like mini-focus shifts or talking to yourself in the third person can offer quick relief.
12. In social settings, plan ahead to handle restlessness so you do not feel overwhelmed.

Conclusion

Worry and restlessness can strike at any time, threatening to derail the progress you have made. By recognizing signs early, setting routines, and using both basic and advanced calming methods, you can greatly reduce the hold these feelings have over you. You have many tools at your disposal—from breathing exercises to supportive chats with trusted individuals.

In the next chapter, we will explore how to fortify your connections with the people around you. Healthy ties can serve as a steady base when worry or other challenging emotions arise. By combining the tips you have learned so far with strong, supportive relationships, you can safeguard your mental well-being and keep harmful habits from taking hold again.

CHAPTER 5: STRENGTHENING CONNECTIONS WITH OTHERS

Introduction
People often say it takes a network of trusted connections to support mental health after breaking harmful habits. Strong bonds with others can make you feel understood and less alone. Whether these connections are with family, friends, or supportive groups, feeling linked to others can keep you steady when life gets tough.

In this chapter, we will explore ways to improve your relationships, handle conflict, and find new connections if your old circles are not healthy. We will look at how to share your feelings and needs in a direct way, and we will examine what to do if someone close to you is not ready to offer help or respect your limits. By the end of this chapter, you will have a range of practical ideas for building healthier, more satisfying connections with people who matter to you.

5.1 Understanding Why Connections Matter

A sense of belonging is a basic human need. During addiction, ties with others might have been damaged. You might have lied, broken promises, or hurt people without meaning to. Once you decide to change, building or rebuilding trust with others can be a real challenge. However, it is important for several reasons:

- **Emotional Support**: Sharing problems with someone can lower stress. Feeling heard helps you realize that you do not have to solve everything alone.
- **Accountability**: People who care about you can also help you stay on track by noticing changes in your behavior or mood before you do.
- **Learning from Others**: In a healthy group, you learn tips and strategies you might never have considered on your own.

5.2 Choosing People Who Support Your Health

Not everyone you meet will help you grow in a safe way. Some might lead you back to your old habits. So, how do you figure out who is good for you?

1. **Look at Their Actions**: Do they respect your boundaries and choices? Do they keep pushing harmful substances or negative behaviors on you?
2. **Check Your Mood Around Them**: Do you feel drained, anxious, or worthless after spending time together? Or do you feel encouraged and calm?
3. **See If They Listen**: A true supporter will let you speak and try to understand your point of view instead of making every conversation about themselves.

By noticing these signs, you can decide who might be a good partner in your healing and who might be safer to avoid.

5.3 Rebuilding Relationships with Family

Family ties can be complicated. Some family members might have seen you at your worst, and there can be unresolved anger or disappointment on both sides. Here are some tips to mend or maintain family connections:

- **Honest Talks**: Sometimes, you need a calm and open talk about what happened in the past. Apologize if you caused harm, but also explain that you are working on a new path.
- **Give Them Time**: Even if you change your actions now, your family might still feel worried or skeptical. Try not to rush their acceptance. Show them through your consistent behavior that you are different.
- **Set Limits if Needed**: Some family members might be toxic or unsupportive. If they continue to put you down or bring harmful elements into your life, you might need to limit contact for your own safety.

5.4 Improving Friendship Circles

Your old group of friends might have been linked to the harmful habits you quit. So, you might ask: should you keep them in your life, or move on and find new peers?

- **Assess Shared Interests**: If your only common ground was the old behavior, you might not have much in common anymore. It could be time to explore new groups that share healthier interests.
- **Explain Your Needs**: If you want to remain friends, tell them clearly that you have changed your focus. Let them know what activities are off-limits for you now. A real friend should be able to respect that.
- **Stay Open to New People**: You do not have to make a best friend overnight, but try joining local activities, online communities (focused on helpful subjects), or support groups. That way, you can find people who understand your new goals.

5.5 Communication That Builds Trust

Even in your closest relationships, communication can break down if you feel misunderstood or judged. Strengthening your connections usually starts with better communication skills. Consider these methods:

1. **Use "I" Statements**: Instead of saying, "You make me angry," try, "I feel angry when this happens because…" This prevents others from feeling attacked.
2. **Practice Active Listening**: When the other person is speaking, show that you are listening by giving small nods or saying, "I see," or "I understand." Then, repeat back what you heard to confirm you got it right.
3. **Stay on Topic**: If you are upset about a specific issue, focus on that issue alone. Avoid bringing up every past mistake or annoyance in the same conversation. This keeps the discussion clear and more likely to lead to a solution.

5.6 Resolving Conflicts in a Healthy Way

Arguments will happen, no matter how well you get along. But if you handle conflicts in a more controlled way, they can help you understand each other rather than tear your bond apart.

- **Calm Down First**: If you are too angry or upset, take a break before talking. Otherwise, you might say something hurtful you do not really mean.

- **Define the Real Problem**: Try to name exactly what is bothering you. Is it that someone did not respect your limit, or that you felt ignored during a key moment? Clarifying the issue helps to fix it.
- **Seek Middle Ground**: If possible, suggest a small compromise. Maybe you both adjust your actions slightly. Each side feels heard and is more likely to honor the agreement.

5.7 Handling Rejection or Negative Reactions

Sometimes, you might try to fix a relationship or connect with someone new, and they are not interested or they respond harshly. This can hurt, especially if you are trying hard to change. Here is how to cope:

1. **Accept Their Choice**: You cannot force someone to trust or like you. Recognize that everyone is free to say no.
2. **Avoid Taking It Too Personally**: They might be dealing with their own problems and not have the space to give you a chance.
3. **Learn from It**: If many people react negatively, consider if there is something in your approach that comes across as too pushy or if you need more time to show that you are consistent in your new behavior.

5.8 Advanced Ways to Grow Closer in Support Groups

Support groups (online or local) can be great for sharing experiences with those who have walked a similar road. To get the most out of these communities:

- **Attend Regularly**: Being present at weekly or monthly meetings helps you build trust and familiarity.
- **Participate Respectfully**: Listen without interrupting. When it is your turn, speak honestly.
- **Exchange Contact Info Carefully**: If you feel a bond with someone, you can stay in touch between meetings. However, be mindful of boundaries. Make sure both sides are comfortable sharing personal information.

5.9 Giving and Receiving Help

A strong bond is not just about taking help from others. It also involves offering support when you can:

- **Offer Genuine Support**: Ask how someone is doing. Offer to help in small ways if they seem stressed—like listening to them for a few minutes or sharing a tip that worked for you.
- **Respect Your Own Limits**: If a friend's problem is too heavy or triggers your own fears, you do not have to handle it alone. Suggest they speak to a counselor or a group that specializes in that issue.
- **Avoid "Fixing" Them**: Sometimes, people just need to talk. You do not have to solve every detail. Instead, you can listen and show understanding.

5.10 How to Talk About Your Recovery

Some people in your life might not know the details of your addiction or how it affected you. Deciding what and how to share can be tricky:

- **Consider the Relationship**: You might tell your closest friends or family more details than you would share with a casual acquaintance.
- **Be Brief but Honest**: You do not have to share your entire history. A short explanation like, "I struggled with something harmful, and now I'm working hard to stay healthy," can be enough for many people.
- **Focus on the Present**: If people push for details you are not ready to share, bring the conversation back to the present. You can say, "I'm focusing on what I can do to keep growing in a safer way right now."

5.11 Setting Boundaries with Others

Boundaries are rules you create to protect your mental and emotional space. They can be hard to define if you are used to putting everyone else first. Here are some steps to form and keep boundaries:

1. **Decide What Is Not Okay**: Maybe you do not allow anyone to bring certain substances into your home, or you refuse to be around constant complaining.

2. **Communicate Clearly**: Tell people what your boundaries are. For instance, "I need you to call before dropping by" or "I cannot hang out if you plan to drink."
3. **Enforce Consequences**: If someone keeps crossing the line, you might need to leave the situation or limit your time with them. Consistency shows you mean what you say.

5.12 Using Technology to Stay Connected Safely

In the modern world, technology can help you maintain or grow connections—but it can also be a source of stress if misused. Keep these tips in mind:

- **Online Support Groups**: If you cannot join a local group, online communities or video meetings can offer shared experiences and tips.
- **Set Time Limits**: Endless scrolling can lead to comparing yourself with others or other forms of negativity. Choose certain times of day to check your messages, and then step away.
- **Avoid Hostile Interactions**: If someone is argumentative or rude on social media, do not engage. You can block or mute them. Protecting your peace is more important than winning an online argument.

5.13 Recognizing When You Need Outside Mediation

Sometimes, a relationship problem is too big for simple do-it-yourself solutions. You might need a neutral third person, like a counselor, religious leader, or mediator:

- **Family Counseling**: If your household is full of tension, a trained counselor can guide everyone to speak more safely and find real solutions.
- **Couples Therapy**: If you have a partner, professional help can resolve deep issues, especially if your old addiction put a strain on the relationship.

- **Conflict Resolution Services**: Some communities offer free or low-cost mediation for disputes that seem stuck. Having a neutral listener can help both sides calm down and talk productively.

5.14 Protecting Your Mental Health in Large Social Events

Weddings, birthdays, or big family gatherings can be overwhelming, especially if you are still building confidence in your social skills. Here are some pointers:

- **Plan Ahead**: Ask who will be there, what kind of activities will happen, and whether substances will be present.
- **Have an Exit Plan**: If you start feeling stressed, it is okay to leave early. Arrange your own transportation if possible, so you are not stuck.
- **Choose a Buddy**: Bring a supportive friend or talk to a family member who is ready to help you manage any tense moments.

5.15 Less-Known Methods to Strengthen Bonds

Here are some special ideas that can help you connect with others in ways you might not have tried before:

1. **Shared Projects**: Instead of just chatting, work on a small task or project together, such as cooking a new recipe or painting a room. Shared achievements can create deeper trust.
2. **Listening Exercises**: Ask a friend to describe something important to them for five minutes, and you only listen. Then switch. This simple activity can improve understanding on both sides.
3. **Weekly Check-Ins**: If you have someone you trust, agree to do a quick weekly text or call to share how you are feeling. This can keep you both honest and present in each other's lives.

5.16 When to Step Back from a Relationship

Not every relationship can be healed. At times, the kindest thing for yourself is to let go or maintain distance:

- **Continuous Harm**: If someone is verbally abusive or uses your past struggles to mock you, you have the right to disconnect for your own safety.
- **Relentless Pressure to Use**: Friends or family who keep forcing old habits on you are risky. Letting them go might hurt, but it can protect your new, healthier lifestyle.
- **Repeated Disrespect of Boundaries**: If you have stated your limits clearly and the person ignores them over and over, consider limiting or ending contact.

5.17 Building a Team of Healthy Relationships

Instead of relying on just one person, try to develop a small group of people who support your recovery from different angles:

- **Emotional Allies**: A friend or family member who listens without blame when you need to talk about feelings.
- **Practical Allies**: Someone who can help with real-life tasks or advice, like finding work, applying for school, or dealing with paperwork.
- **Recovery Allies**: A mentor, sponsor, or group buddy who understands the ins and outs of addiction and can offer steady guidance when you feel shaky.

Having a few different supporters can reduce the burden on any single person and give you more varied insights.

5.18 Key Points from Chapter 5

1. Feeling connected to others is important for emotional support, accountability, and learning new tips.
2. Not everyone is a healthy influence. Observe how you feel around people and decide who strengthens your progress.
3. Family ties can be rebuilt with honest talks, apologies if needed, and patience, but you must also set limits if the environment is toxic.
4. New friends may be needed if old friends are tied to harmful behaviors.

5. Good communication includes "I" statements, active listening, and staying on topic.
6. Conflict can be helpful if managed calmly and clearly.
7. You cannot force someone to connect with you; respect their choice if they say no.
8. Support groups (online or offline) can offer fresh perspectives.
9. Sharing your own story in a way that feels comfortable can deepen understanding.
10. Boundaries protect your emotional space and need to be clearly stated and enforced.
11. Technology can help you stay connected but limit time spent on social media.
12. Outside mediation or counseling can save relationships that are stuck in conflict.
13. Large social events require planning to avoid feeling trapped or triggered.
14. Projects, listening exercises, and weekly check-ins are unique ways to grow closer to people.
15. In some cases, stepping away from harmful relationships is the best choice.
16. Build a small support team with emotional, practical, and recovery-focused allies.

Conclusion

Connections with others can lift you up when you feel discouraged and keep you anchored during uncertain times. By choosing healthy influences, improving communication skills, and knowing when to step away from toxic relationships, you give yourself the best chance at staying on your new path.

In the next chapter, we will explore how to plan a safe future. You will learn how to set realistic goals, manage your environment, and create a backup strategy in case challenges arise. By pairing strong relationships with a smart approach to life planning, you can move forward with steady confidence.

CHAPTER 6: PLANNING A SAFE FUTURE

Introduction
Early recovery often involves focusing on the day in front of you. However, as you gain stability, it is helpful to look ahead. Planning a safe future means making decisions and setting goals that protect your progress and guide you toward a better life. It includes choosing the right job or training path, managing finances more carefully, and designing a living environment that lowers your risk of relapse.

In this chapter, we will talk about practical steps for building a safer tomorrow. We will also look at how to stay flexible because life changes can happen anytime. A plan does not guarantee perfection, but it helps you remain grounded and lowers the chance of being caught off guard by stress or triggers.

6.1 Clarifying What "Safe Future" Means

A safe future does not mean hiding from the world or never taking chances. It means having a life setup that reduces the appeal or likelihood of returning to harmful behaviors. This can include:

- **Stable Work or School**: Having daily responsibilities can bring structure and a sense of purpose.
- **Healthy Surroundings**: Living in a place where you do not face daily exposure to substances or destructive influences.
- **Financial Security**: Avoiding constant money stress, which can be a major relapse trigger.

At the same time, building a safe future allows for personal growth. You still try new things and take on challenges, but you do so in a way that supports your mental well-being.

6.2 Setting Realistic Goals

When planning, it is easy to dream big: "I want to run my own company," or "I want to travel everywhere." While big goals can inspire you, it is important to break them down into smaller steps:

1. **Break Down the Goal**: If you want a certain career, list what you need first: a diploma, specific training, or a skill set.
2. **Check Your Timeline**: Decide when you can realistically reach each step. Avoid rushing. Too much pressure can harm your mental state.
3. **Reward Progress**: Each time you complete a step, acknowledge your effort. It keeps you motivated to continue.

6.3 Building a Supportive Daily Routine

A well-structured day can protect you from boredom, worry, or impulsive decisions that could lead to relapse. Consider these elements:

- **Regular Wake-Up Time**: Start your day at a set time. This helps your body clock stay steady.
- **Task Blocks**: Divide your day into blocks for work, meals, rest, and leisure activities. Write it down or use a planner if it helps.
- **Review Evenings**: Spend a few minutes at the end of each day checking what you did. If something triggered stress, note it down so you can address it.

6.4 Planning for Financial Security

Money troubles can cause worry, shame, or desperation, all of which can drive people back to harmful habits. Here are some steps to handle finances more safely:

- **Basic Budgeting**: Write down your monthly income and list your expenses: rent, bills, groceries, and so on. Compare to see if you need to adjust spending.
- **Emergency Fund**: Even setting aside a small amount each week can help. Over time, this can become a cushion for unexpected events.
- **Avoid Overuse of Credit**: Credit cards or loans can be tempting, but piling up debt can lead to high stress.

If finances are a large struggle, look for local financial counseling services or free online courses that teach money basics.

6.5 Choosing a Healthy Living Environment

If your living space is full of triggers—like old friends who still use, or easy access to harmful substances—staying on a safer path becomes tough. Think about:

- **Location**: Do you live in a neighborhood that reminds you of old ways, or is close to places you used to visit when you were stuck in addiction? Consider moving if possible, or find ways to avoid those areas.
- **Housemates**: Living with people who respect your recovery is key. If you share space with someone who frequently uses harmful substances, it might be time to rethink your arrangement.
- **Clean and Organized Space**: A cluttered environment can add stress. Keeping a tidy home or room can help you feel more in control.

6.6 Handling Work or School Pressures

Stress from work or school can be a big problem if you do not manage it well. You can make it safer by:

1. **Setting Clear Boundaries**: If your boss or teachers expect too much, learn to say, "I cannot take on more right now."
2. **Time Management**: Plan your assignments or work tasks to avoid last-minute panic. Breaking large projects into parts can reduce anxiety.
3. **Asking for Help**: If you feel overwhelmed, talk to a manager, teacher, or counselor about possible solutions, such as extended deadlines or job adjustments.

Having a supportive work or study environment increases your chance of staying on track.

6.7 Backup Plans for Stressful Times

No matter how careful you are, life can throw surprises at you. A key part of a safe future is having backup plans for when life gets messy:

- **Stress-Busting Tactics**: Know which coping methods work best for you (breathing exercises, calling a friend, stepping outdoors). Use them at the first sign of trouble.
- **Temporary Housing Options**: If your living situation becomes unsafe, do you have a friend, relative, or shelter you can go to for a short time?
- **Support Contact List**: Keep a list of phone numbers for local hotlines, sponsors, or supportive friends in an easy-to-reach place.

6.8 Balancing Goals with Real-Life Demands

Sometimes people want to achieve so many things at once—get a new job, repair every relationship, pay off debt—that they become overwhelmed. Balancing ambition with practical limits is crucial:

- **Prioritize**: Pick one main goal to focus on at a time, such as stabilizing your income or finishing a training course. Once you make good progress, you can add the next goal.
- **Check Your Energy**: If you are feeling run-down or anxious, it could be a sign that you are pushing yourself too hard. Slow down and make time for rest.
- **Celebrate Small Wins**: Simple actions like finishing a class module or creating a workable budget plan are worth noticing. Recognizing these steps helps you stay motivated.

6.9 The Power of Mentors or Guides

Sometimes, having someone who has walked a similar path can make planning easier. This person can be a mentor or guide who offers wisdom you might not get from a general self-help book:

- **Finding a Mentor**: Look in your local recovery group or ask around. Some people have experience with both addiction and rebuilding their lives in a certain field (like business, art, or trades).

- **Asking the Right Questions**: Instead of saying, "Tell me everything," you can ask, "How did you handle setbacks in work or school?" or "What helped you most when you felt like giving up?"
- **Keeping It Mutual**: Over time, you might find ways to help your mentor as well. Healthy relationships involve give and take, even if you have different experiences.

6.10 Dealing with Unexpected Changes

Life can shift in ways you did not predict. Maybe a job offer falls through, or a family member needs sudden help. When unexpected events happen:

1. **Pause and Assess**: Instead of panicking, see what options exist. Is there another job you can apply for quickly? Can other family members share the load of helping?
2. **Adjust Your Goals**: You might need to change your timeline or rearrange priorities. That is okay. Flexibility is part of a safe plan.
3. **Seek Extra Support**: During major changes, it might help to speak with a counselor or a trusted friend. Getting a new perspective can calm anxiety.

6.11 Involving Loved Ones in Your Future Plans

If you have a partner, close friend, or family member you trust, letting them know about your goals can create a team effort:

- **Explain Your Reasons**: For instance, tell them why choosing a certain career path or moving to a new place is important to you.
- **Ask for Input**: They might see risks or solutions that you missed. But remember, final decisions are yours to make.
- **Agree on Boundaries**: If they want to help, clarify what kind of help is actually useful. Maybe you appreciate them checking in on you once a week, but not every day.

6.12 Keeping Healthy Habits to Protect Your Future

Physical health and mental health are closely linked. If you neglect your body, your mind becomes more vulnerable to stress, which can threaten your safe future:

- **Basic Nutrition**: Aim to include fruits, vegetables, protein, and enough water in your daily intake.
- **Consistent Sleep Schedule**: Enough rest helps your brain manage stress better.
- **Simple Exercise Routine**: Even a daily 10-minute walk can support a clearer mind.

These habits lower the chances of being overrun by anxiety or sadness, which can make you vulnerable to relapse.

6.13 Finding Enjoyable Hobbies and Activities

Planning a safe future does not have to feel like a chore. Adding fun activities can give you something to look forward to:

- **Explore New Interests**: Consider affordable classes, sports clubs, or art groups in your area.
- **Creative Outlets**: Writing, painting, or making music can relax your mind and offer a healthy distraction from negative thoughts.
- **Meaningful Social Outings**: Schedule events or small get-togethers with supportive friends. Staying involved with positive people guards you against loneliness.

6.14 Checking for Possible Risks in Your Plan

Before you settle on a path, do a quick risk check:

- **Work Risks**: Will your job put you in contact with people who use harmful substances, or is it a high-stress role that might overwhelm you quickly?

- **Emotional Risks**: Are you about to move back to a place where you once had a lot of negative memories? Could that trigger old feelings?
- **Time Commitment**: Do you have enough time for the training or job you plan to pursue? If it crowds out sleep or personal care, it might not be safe for your mental health.

6.15 Special Tips You Might Not Have Heard

Here are a few advanced ideas that can give you an extra layer of protection as you plan your future:

1. **Volunteer in a Field of Interest**: Doing volunteer work in a place that connects to your future goal can help you learn the ropes without the full pressure of paid employment. You gain skills and references along the way.
2. **Future Self Letters**: Write a letter to yourself about where you want to be in six months or a year. Keep it safe, and read it on the target date. It can show you how far you have come and if you need to adjust your direction.
3. **"What If" Scenarios**: In a journal, write down a few possible setbacks (like losing a job) and brainstorm at least two ways you could respond. This practice trains your mind to stay calm during real crises.

6.16 Practicing Mindfulness During Planning

When you are planning goals, it is easy to get lost in "what if" thoughts and get anxious about the future. Staying mindful can help:

- **Take It Step by Step**: Focus on what you need to do today or this week. Avoid letting your mind jump too far ahead.
- **Be Present in Research**: If you are searching for job postings or studying a new skill, give that task your full attention.
- **Self-Check for Stress**: If you notice your shoulders tensing or your jaw clenching, pause. Take a few slow breaths, then continue.

6.17 Balancing Independence and Help

You might feel excited to prove you can handle life on your own, especially if you have had people doubt you in the past. But do not let pride keep you from using available resources:

- **Government or Community Support**: Many places have free or low-cost programs for education, healthcare, or job training.
- **Recovery Centers**: Some recovery programs offer ongoing workshops or skill-building sessions.
- **Trusted Friends**: If a friend offers to help you practice job interviews or read over your resume, consider accepting. Collaboration does not mean you are weak.

6.18 Key Points from Chapter 6

1. A safe future involves having a stable job or school path, healthy surroundings, and a financial plan that lowers stress.
2. Breaking large goals into smaller steps stops you from feeling swamped.
3. A daily routine, with set times for waking and tasks, builds a strong structure for life.
4. Handling finances wisely includes budgeting, saving a little each week, and being careful with credit.
5. Living in a stable environment can mean avoiding high-risk neighborhoods or moving away from harmful housemates.
6. Work or school pressures can be lessened by clear communication, time management, and asking for help when needed.
7. Backup plans for sudden changes can keep you from being thrown off balance.
8. Use mentors or guides who have navigated similar challenges.
9. Unexpected changes might require adjusting your goals rather than giving up.
10. Talk to people you trust about your plans, but remember that you decide what is best for you.
11. Healthy habits like good nutrition, rest, and light exercise protect your mental health.

12. Adding fun hobbies and social events keeps you motivated and reduces isolation.
13. Check for any hidden risks in your plan, such as triggers tied to a certain job or location.
14. Advanced tips like volunteering in your chosen field, writing future self letters, or drafting "What If" scenarios can give you a stronger safety net.
15. Mindfulness keeps you focused on the tasks at hand and reduces anxiety about the future.
16. Mixing self-reliance with available help can increase your chances of success.

Conclusion
Planning a safe future is about building an environment where you can thrive without needing harmful crutches. By setting practical goals, choosing a healthy space to live and work, and staying prepared for life's sudden changes, you lower the risk of sliding back into old habits. You also give yourself a real chance to achieve dreams that once seemed out of reach.

In the next chapter, you will learn about transforming harmful thoughts. Sometimes, internal negative chatter can be the biggest threat to long-term health. You will find tactics to identify and replace self-defeating thoughts with more balanced and supportive ones, making your mind a safer place to be.

CHAPTER 7: TRANSFORMING HARMFUL THOUGHTS

Introduction
Many people find that quitting a harmful habit is only the beginning. Even if you no longer use a substance or behavior that once had a hold on you, the thoughts in your mind might still be sharp and unkind. Some thoughts can trigger guilt, shame, or hopelessness. Others might urge you to return to risky behavior, even if you know it is not the best choice. In this chapter, you will learn how to identify and change harmful thoughts into safer, more balanced views.

We will explore simple strategies to catch negative self-talk, as well as more advanced ideas that can give you extra control over your own thinking. You will not need fancy or complex words to use these ideas. Instead, you can focus on plain, practical steps that help you handle your thoughts in calmer ways. By learning to transform harmful thoughts, you can protect your emotional well-being and stay on a steady path of growth.

7.1 What Are Harmful Thoughts?

A harmful thought can be any idea or pattern in your mind that worsens your stress or pushes you toward actions that are not good for you. These thoughts might appear suddenly, or they might quietly linger in the back of your mind. Below are some common forms:

1. **Self-Criticism**: "I always fail," or "I am not good enough." These statements ignore facts about your strengths or the progress you have already made.
2. **Worst-Case Beliefs**: "It will all go wrong," or "I will never fix this." This sort of thinking imagines only the most negative outcomes, without evidence.
3. **Unrealistic Expectations**: "I should be perfect by now," or "I must do everything right or I have failed." Such rigid standards can cause constant stress.
4. **Regret and Shame**: "I cannot believe I did those things; I am a bad person forever." While it is normal to feel regret for past actions, endlessly punishing yourself can stunt healthy growth.

Not every harmful thought is obvious. Some slip in as subtle beliefs that shape your mood and your actions. Identifying them is the first step to neutralizing their impact.

7.2 Why Harmful Thoughts Persist

You might wonder why these thoughts keep appearing, even when you try to move forward. There are several reasons they can linger:

- **Habit Formation**: If you spent years thinking you were worthless or hopeless, your mind might repeat these thoughts out of habit.
- **Past Conditioning**: Family or friends may have labeled you in negative ways, and you absorbed those beliefs without questioning them.
- **Brain Chemistry**: Periods of extreme stress, poor sleep, or emotional imbalance can make it easier for negative beliefs to take root.
- **Fear of Change**: Sometimes, part of you might believe these thoughts are protecting you from new risks. For example, if you think you will fail anyway, you might avoid trying new things, which removes the risk of disappointment.

Realizing that harmful thoughts can be part of old mental patterns or the result of stress does not fix everything, but it does show you that these thoughts are not always telling the truth.

7.3 Spotting Harmful Thoughts Early

The sooner you notice a negative or distorted idea in your mind, the easier it is to do something about it. Here are simple ways to spot them:

1. **Track Changes in Mood**: If your mood suddenly drops, pause and ask what you were just thinking. Often, a burst of sadness or stress is triggered by a quick, negative thought.
2. **Listen for Key Phrases**: Words like "never," "always," or "can't" often indicate a harmful idea. For example, "I will never be happy again."

3. **Write Them Down**: Keep a small notebook or use a basic note app to jot down any strong or troubling thought. This helps you see patterns over time.

Once you are aware of these thoughts, you can step back and decide if they are factual or if they are simply mental habits.

7.4 Basic Methods to Shift Your Thinking

If you catch yourself in a harmful thought, these simple methods can help you steer toward a more balanced view:

1. **Ask for Proof**: When a harsh statement pops up, ask, "Is there real proof?" For example, if you think, "I cannot do anything right," remind yourself of a time you handled a task well or overcame a problem.
2. **Use Softer Words**: Change absolute words like "never" or "always" to "sometimes" or "this time." Even a small shift in wording can cut down on the drama of the thought.
3. **Short Rebuttal**: If your mind says, "I am sure to fail," answer with, "I will do my best, and that might be good enough."

These small interventions may not fix your mood instantly, but they can stop negative ideas from growing stronger.

7.5 Advanced Strategies for Transforming Harmful Beliefs

Sometimes basic questioning is not enough. Certain thoughts can be stubborn and keep coming back. In these cases, it can help to use more advanced tools:

1. **Name the Thought**: Give a brief name to the negative mindset, like "the blame voice" or "the panic channel." By labeling it, you separate it from your core self.
2. **Distance Technique**: Speak to the thought in your mind as if it is an outside factor. For instance, "I see you, fear. You are saying I will fail. I hear you, but I am choosing to keep going."

3. **Repeat with Caution**: Sometimes, hearing a negative thought on purpose, out loud, can drain its power. For instance, if your mind says, "You are doomed," you might say it aloud five times in a plain, bored tone until it sounds silly. This will not work for everyone, but some people find it reduces the thought's effect.

7.6 Replacing Harmful Thought Patterns with Healthier Ones

It is not enough to simply remove negative beliefs; you also want to replace them with ideas that help you stay calm and confident. Below are suggestions:

- **Gratitude Check**: Each day, list a few things you are thankful for. This helps your mind look for positive details rather than negative ones.
- **Visual Reminders**: Put short, supportive statements or images where you will see them, like on your phone's background or near your bed.
- **Positive Data Collection**: Each time you handle a tough moment well, note it down. Later, when your mind says you cannot do anything right, you have proof that you can handle challenges.

Replacing old patterns takes time, but with repetition, your mind can learn to lean on these healthier beliefs more often.

7.7 Handling Guilt and Shame Thoughts

Feelings of guilt and shame are common after a period of harmful behavior. While guilt can push you to make amends or do better, too much guilt or ongoing shame can lead to hopelessness. Here are some ways to handle these specific thoughts:

1. **Separate the Act from the Person**: For example, "I did something harmful, but I am willing to grow." This allows you to own your mistake without labeling yourself as a worthless person.
2. **Make Amends When Possible**: If it is safe and respectful, consider apologizing or taking action to fix the damage you caused. This can ease some of the ongoing negative self-talk.

3. **Limit Dwelling on the Past**: Remind yourself that you are focusing on safer actions now. Repeatedly beating yourself up does not undo what happened; it only harms your progress in the present.

7.8 How Thoughts Tie into Urges or Cravings

Sometimes, your mind might use negative ideas as a gateway to old habits. For example, "I have messed everything up, so I might as well go back to the old behavior." Recognizing this pattern is crucial:

- **Spot the Craving Thought**: "One more time won't hurt," or "This is too hard; my old habit is easier."
- **Interrupt with Truth**: Recall the real harm that old habits caused. Note any serious problems that might happen if you return to them.
- **Use a Replacement Activity**: Keep your mind busy with a healthier task, like making a phone call to someone supportive, going for a safe walk, or doing a simple puzzle.

Being watchful of how negative thoughts can encourage cravings helps you respond quickly and avoid falling back into risky behavior.

7.9 Thoughts That Arise from Stress or Tiredness

Stress and fatigue can make harmful thoughts louder. When you are exhausted, small problems seem huge. When you are under stress, your mind might assume everything is going downhill. You can fight this in a few ways:

1. **Basic Self-Care**: Ensure you get enough rest, proper food, and some movement each day. A healthy body supports a clearer mind.
2. **Pause in Stressful Times**: Before letting harmful thoughts spiral, step back. Ask yourself if you are tired or hungry. Sometimes, meeting a simple need can lower stress enough to think clearly.
3. **Schedule Breaks**: If you have a busy life, plan short breaks where you do a calming action, like breathing or quietly resting your mind. This can prevent a buildup of stress that fuels negative ideas.

7.10 Peer and Group Support for Harmful Thoughts

Discussing your negative thoughts with others might feel embarrassing at first. But many people who have quit harmful habits go through the same struggles. Connecting with a support group or a trusted friend can help:

- **Shared Experience**: Hearing someone say, "I used to think that way, too," can be a big relief.
- **Encouragement to Challenge the Thought**: Someone else might have a tip or phrase you never considered for disputing a harmful belief.
- **Building Hope**: Seeing people who have succeeded in stopping negative self-talk can show you that real change is possible.

7.11 Keeping a Thought Journal

One of the most direct tools for understanding your mind is a thought journal. Here is how you can keep one:

1. **Basic Layout**: Draw a simple table with columns for the situation, the thought, and a realistic response.
2. **Write in It Often**: Whether it is once a day or after a stressful event, consistent use helps you track progress.
3. **Review Weekly**: Look back and see if certain thoughts keep showing up. With this insight, you can create strategies to handle them faster.

A thought journal does not have to be pretty or perfect. It just needs to capture key details so you can see your patterns clearly.

7.12 Techniques to Use When Thoughts Feel Out of Control

Sometimes, harmful thoughts come in strong waves. You might feel as though you cannot stop them. If this happens:

- **Grounding in the Present**: Name a few things you see around you, or listen for different sounds. Force your mind to notice details in your current surroundings instead of following the negative spiral.

- **Count a Sequence**: Recite a simple pattern, like counting backward from 30, or listing the months of the year in reverse. This forces the thinking part of your brain to engage, cutting off the negative stream.
- **Seek Immediate Help**: If your mind is telling you to harm yourself or to do something dangerous, reach out to a trusted person or contact a mental health hotline. Taking action quickly can prevent a crisis.

7.13 Less Common Ideas for Transforming Thought Patterns

Below are some specialized methods you might not see in basic guides:

1. **Talk-Back Method with an Object**: Some people find it helpful to set an empty chair or a pillow in front of them and speak to it as though it represents the harmful thought. This can help you voice your concerns and practice your counter-arguments out loud.
2. **Use Humor**: If you can safely find something funny in an extreme statement your mind makes, it can break tension. For example, if your mind says, "Today is doomed," you might imagine a cartoon version of a silly doom day. Humor can lessen the power of fear.
3. **Break the Visual**: If you see harsh images in your head, change the color or shape of them in your mind. Turn a dark scene into something oddly colored or shrink it down. Simple mental tricks like these can reduce the emotional intensity.

7.14 Working with a Counselor or Therapist

While many can do a lot on their own to combat harmful thoughts, sometimes professional help is the best route:

- **Guided Thought Analysis**: Therapists can teach you structured ways to question harmful beliefs that you may not learn on your own.
- **Safety Plans**: If your thoughts lean toward self-harm, a counselor can help you create a plan for dangerous situations.
- **Deep-Level Work**: Some thoughts might have roots in trauma or deeply set patterns from childhood. A counselor can provide a safe space to address these issues.

You do not have to stay in therapy forever, but even a short series of sessions can give you powerful tools for your mind.

7.15 Thoughts Linked to Regaining Self-Worth

Harmful thoughts often involve low self-worth. You might feel like you cannot do better or do not deserve good things in life. Here are ways to remind yourself that you have worth:

1. **List Achievements**: They do not have to be grand. Even small wins like cooking a meal, cleaning your room, or helping a friend show you are capable.
2. **Self-Respect in Daily Life**: Think about how you dress, how you hold yourself, and how you speak. Small acts of self-care and respect can influence your inner talk.
3. **Positive Role Models**: Find stories or people who overcame similar obstacles. Seeing them treat themselves with care can inspire you to think better of yourself, too.

7.16 Making New Pathways in the Mind

Scientists talk about "pathways" in the brain. When you think the same way over and over, that pathway grows stronger. To change this, you create new thought patterns and repeat them:

- **Practice Repetition**: Each time you catch a harmful thought and respond with a helpful phrase, you strengthen a new pathway.
- **Stay Patient**: These mental roads do not form overnight. Expect to put in daily effort for weeks or months before noticing major results.
- **Reward Yourself**: When you successfully shift from a harmful idea to a healthier one, give yourself a mental pat on the back. Recognizing each small step can keep you motivated.

7.17 Setting Specific Goals for Thought Control

Like any other change, altering your thinking can benefit from defined targets:

1. **One Thought Type at a Time**: Pick a specific negative pattern you want to reduce, like "I am worthless." Focus on that for a week or two, practicing your counters regularly.
2. **Measure Frequency**: You might note how many times a day the harmful thought appears. Over time, see if this number goes down.
3. **Reward System**: Decide on a small treat (like reading a few pages of a favorite book or taking a short rest outside) when you stay aware of your harmful thoughts and respond calmly.

7.18 Key Points from Chapter 7

1. Harmful thoughts are patterns of thinking that cause stress, guilt, or lead to risky behavior.
2. These thoughts often show up due to habit, past conditioning, or stress.
3. Spot them early by noticing mood changes, using a thought journal, and looking for words like "never" or "always."
4. Basic shifts include asking for proof, softening extreme words, and offering yourself a short rebuttal.
5. Advanced strategies involve naming the negative voice or speaking to the thought as if it is an outside factor.
6. Replacing harmful patterns requires daily practice of gratitude, positive data collection, or other simple methods that refocus your mind.
7. Guilt and shame can be managed by separating the act from your identity and, if possible, making amends.
8. Negative beliefs can fuel urges or cravings, so be ready to catch and counter those thoughts quickly.
9. Stress and tiredness can make these thoughts worse, so basic self-care and timely breaks help protect your mind.
10. Thought journals, group support, or talking with a counselor can provide guidance when you feel stuck.
11. Techniques like humor, visualization changes, or talking to an object can reduce the intensity of a harsh inner voice.

12. Building self-worth involves small daily achievements, self-respect, and positive influences.
13. Changing your thinking takes time, but each time you respond to a harmful idea in a healthier way, you strengthen new mental pathways.
14. Setting specific goals for thought control can help you track progress and stay motivated.

Conclusion

Your mind can be your ally or your biggest challenge, especially after leaving behind an addictive habit. By learning to observe and transform harmful ideas, you gain more power over your own well-being. This chapter introduced a variety of simple and advanced approaches to deal with negative beliefs. They all share a common theme: greater awareness, consistent practice, and self-kindness.

Next, in Chapter 8, we will shift our focus to practical activities that support both mind and body. You will learn ideas to keep yourself active, balanced, and less prone to mental overload. Combining the skills from this chapter with those upcoming physical and mental practices will help you build a stronger foundation for continued health.

CHAPTER 8: USEFUL ACTIVITIES FOR THE MIND AND BODY

Introduction

Quitting a harmful habit involves more than just saying "no" to what held you back. It also means finding new ways to fill your time and new actions that help you feel strong, clear-headed, and calm. Working on your mental and physical well-being is key to staying steady in the face of stress. By building a range of safe and useful activities, you create a life where there is less room for old cravings or unhelpful thoughts to take over.

In this chapter, we will discuss simple exercises for your mind and body. You do not need special equipment or high-level skills. The main aim is to find routines that support your body, center your thoughts, and help you grow in safer ways. Whether you prefer indoor or outdoor tasks, group settings or alone time, there will be plenty of practical tips here. By testing different ideas, you can discover which ones fit your life best.

8.1 Why Activities Matter After Harmful Habits

When someone stops using a substance or behavior they were once addicted to, they often discover empty spaces in their day. It is easy to feel bored or restless. Activities that build mental and physical health give you a healthier way to spend that time. Benefits include:

- **Lower Stress and Anxiety**: Many activities help your body produce feel-good chemicals or distract you from worries.
- **Improved Self-Esteem**: Learning new skills or completing tasks can remind you that you are capable of growing.
- **Less Risk of Relapse**: Filling your day with positive actions makes it harder for urges to sneak in.

8.2 Organizing Your Activity Plan

Before we look at specific ideas, it helps to have a basic plan. Consider the following steps:

1. **Check Your Interests**: Are you more drawn to physical exercise, creative projects, or group events? Start with what you like or would like to explore.
2. **Set Time Slots**: Aim for short, regular sessions instead of occasional long marathons. For example, try 30 minutes of an activity each day.
3. **Track Your Feelings**: After each activity, note how you felt. Over time, this will show which ones help the most.

Even if you cannot do big chunks of time, small steps add up.

8.3 Simple Exercises to Keep Your Body Active

You do not need a fancy gym membership to stay active. Here are some beginner-friendly ways to move your body:

1. **Walks at a Steady Pace**: Walking is low-impact and easy to start. Pick a safe neighborhood or a park. Even 15 minutes of steady walking can clear your mind.
2. **Gentle Stretches**: You can stretch your arms, legs, back, and neck each morning or evening. This can improve blood flow and reduce muscle tightness.
3. **Light Home Routines**: Simple exercises like push-ups against a wall, squats using a chair for support, or short sets of calf raises can be done in your living room.

As you grow more comfortable, you can increase the time or try new actions. The key is to stay consistent and listen to your body's signals.

8.4 Breathing Activities for Calmness

Many people underestimate the power of breathing to soothe the mind. After harmful habits, tension can be high, and breathing methods can help you relax:

- **Counting Breaths**: Sit in a calm spot. Inhale slowly while counting to four, hold for one second, then exhale while counting to four. Repeat for a few cycles.

- **Hand on Belly**: Place one hand on your stomach and feel it rise when you inhale. This ensures you are taking deeper breaths, not shallow ones in your chest.
- **Paced Breathing Apps**: You can find simple apps that guide you to breathe at a set pace. Some even show a circle expanding and shrinking, giving you a visual aid.

Regular practice of calm breathing can help you stay grounded, especially during moments of stress.

8.5 Finding a Creative Outlet

Creative activities can give your mind a safe way to express feelings or ideas. This is especially helpful if you are dealing with leftover emotions from past hardships:

1. **Drawing and Doodling**: You do not need to be an artist. Just scribbling shapes or coloring can be soothing.
2. **Writing**: This can be short stories, poems, or even a personal blog. Writing about your feelings can help you see them more clearly.
3. **Crafts**: Knitting, sewing, or making simple models can keep your hands busy and your mind focused on a calm task.

Creative outlets can lower anxiety and offer a sense of achievement, even if no one else ever sees your work.

8.6 Activities for Sharp Thinking

Your mind might still be shifting after leaving a harmful habit. Activities that engage your brain can boost focus and encourage clear thought patterns:

- **Puzzles or Riddles**: Crossword puzzles, word searches, or number puzzles like Sudoku can sharpen your thinking without being too stressful.
- **Reading Non-Fiction**: Pick topics you find interesting. Learning new facts helps your brain stay active and curious.

- **Language Practice**: Free apps or online resources let you pick up new words in a foreign language. This can be a fun daily challenge.

When your mind is busy learning, it has less time to wander toward unhelpful thoughts.

8.7 Adding Social Elements

Being around supportive people can boost the benefits of an activity. If you like the idea of connecting with others:

1. **Group Walks or Community Exercise**: Some neighborhoods have walking clubs or free exercise meetups in local parks.
2. **Book or Craft Clubs**: Joining a club might be a great way to share ideas and stay motivated.
3. **Online Communities**: If leaving home is not easy, you can find online groups. You might attend a virtual meetup where everyone does a puzzle or reads a short story together.

8.8 Music and Movement

Music can lift your mood, and adding simple movement can further help release tension. Consider:

- **Dancing in Private**: Put on a favorite song and move however you like in your living room. This is your time—no one is watching.
- **Drumming on a Table**: Tap out rhythms. This can feel freeing and help you let go of built-up energy.
- **Singing**: Even if you are off-key, singing can lighten your spirit. You could also hum if singing feels too bold.

These small bits of music or rhythm in your day can act like a mental refresh.

8.9 Low-Cost Outdoor Options

If you enjoy being outside, there are many ways to stay active without spending much:

1. **Nature Trails**: Walking along a simple trail can give you fresh air and a sense of peace.
2. **Outdoor Yoga-Style Stretching**: You can stretch on a mat in a quiet park. Just keep the stretches gentle and avoid pressuring yourself to do advanced poses.
3. **Simple Gardening**: Even if you only have a few pots on a balcony or a small yard, taking care of plants can be satisfying. You can grow herbs or small flowers that bring a bit of life to your space.

8.10 Mind Exercises for Relaxation

Beyond breathing, there are other mental practices that can help you slow racing thoughts:

1. **Body Scan**: Close your eyes and slowly move your mind's attention from your toes up to your head, noticing any tension. This can show you where you carry stress.
2. **Basic Visualization**: Imagine a calm place in your mind, such as a quiet beach or a silent forest. Focus on small details. This can give you a short break from worrying thoughts.
3. **Calm Repetition**: Pick a simple word or phrase like "peace" or "I am safe," and repeat it quietly to yourself for a minute or two. The repetition can soothe anxiety.

8.11 Helping Others as an Activity

Sometimes, the best way to boost your own morale is to assist someone else. This can be as simple or as structured as you like:

- **Volunteer Work**: Animal shelters, community kitchens, or youth centers may need extra hands. Even an hour a week can make a difference.

- **Neighborhood Help**: Ask an older neighbor if they need help with groceries or yard tasks. Small acts of kindness can create a sense of belonging.
- **Online Support**: You could join safe forums to share tips with people who are also moving away from harmful habits. Answering questions or offering kind words can remind you of how far you have come.

When you see that your actions help others, it can reinforce the value of the changes you have made in your own life.

8.12 Journaling for Daily Insight

Writing about your day can be more than just tracking thoughts. You can also explore activities, feelings, and plans:

1. **Short Daily Review**: Note what you did, how you felt, and what you learned.
2. **Goal Planning**: List your tasks for tomorrow. This helps your mind rest, knowing you have a plan.
3. **Problem-Solving**: If something bothered you, write about it. Sometimes, writing helps you see a new angle or solution.

Journaling can be a companion to other activities, giving you a record of how they affect your well-being.

8.13 Balancing Solo and Group Activities

There is no single right mix of alone time and social time. Some days, you might want quiet reflection, while on others, you might want company. Consider:

- **Solo Time Benefits**: Peace, self-discovery, and freedom to move at your own pace.
- **Group Time Benefits**: Encouragement, shared experiences, and social bonding.

Try different balances and see how you feel. Both types of activities can help you gain stability in your new, healthier life.

8.14 Less-Known Ways to Keep Mind and Body Engaged

Below are some ideas you might not see in typical self-help guides:

1. **Creative Movement with Objects**: Take something simple like a scarf or small ball and move it around in a pattern that feels interesting or fun. This can soothe restlessness.
2. **Mini Science Experiments**: Simple experiments at home—such as checking how plants grow in different light conditions—can spark curiosity.
3. **Fidget Tools**: Small objects like worry stones or handheld puzzles can keep your hands busy, which can be calming if you often feel edgy.

8.15 Building a Weekly Activity Schedule

One practical step is to create a weekly plan. This does not have to be rigid, but it helps to have a framework:

1. **Choose a Few Main Activities**: Maybe walking, journaling, and a creative hobby. Assign each activity specific days or times.
2. **Allow Flexibility**: If you are feeling too tired or you have an unexpected event, you can move an activity to another day.
3. **Evaluate and Adjust**: After a week or two, decide if the plan is too full or too light. Adjust as needed to match your energy level and interests.

A schedule can keep you from drifting into old patterns of boredom or isolation.

8.16 Coping with Low Motivation Days

Even the best plan might fall apart on days when you feel down or unmotivated. That is normal. You can prepare by:

- **Setting Tiny Targets**: Instead of a 30-minute walk, aim for a 5-minute stroll. Sometimes, just getting started is half the battle.
- **Having "Go-To" Activities**: Pick one or two very easy tasks, like coloring a picture or doing one page of a puzzle. No big effort needed, just enough to keep you from total stagnation.

- **Asking for a Push**: A quick text or call with a supportive friend might give you a small push to try an activity, even if you only manage a short session.

8.17 Checking for Safety and Comfort

When choosing activities, think about your personal limits:

- **Physical Limits**: If you have knee problems, for example, skipping or running might not be best. Find a joint-friendly choice like swimming or slow-paced stretches.
- **Emotional Comfort**: If a group setting makes you very anxious, start with smaller gatherings or online meetups.
- **Financial Safety**: Avoid activities that cost money you do not have. Many low-cost or free options exist, including community resources.

Staying safe and comfortable means you are more likely to keep doing these activities over the long term.

8.18 Key Points from Chapter 8

1. Activities fill your day with healthier actions, lowering the risk of boredom or relapse.
2. A simple plan involves checking your interests, scheduling regular time, and noticing which tasks improve your mood.
3. Body-focused choices include walking, gentle stretches, or light home workouts.
4. Breathing methods calm the mind, while creative outlets help express buried feelings.
5. Activities that sharpen thinking—like puzzles, reading, or learning—can counter unhelpful thoughts.
6. Social activities can provide encouragement, and music or movement can lift mood.
7. Low-cost outdoor tasks like walks in nature or simple gardening are great for fresh air.

8. Mind exercises such as body scans or simple visualization can cut stress quickly.
9. Helping others—through volunteering or small acts of kindness—can boost your own sense of purpose.
10. Journaling gives you daily insights into what works and what challenges you face.
11. A balance of alone time and group experiences can serve different emotional needs.
12. Less-known tricks, such as moving objects in creative patterns or using fidget tools, can settle an uneasy mind.
13. A weekly schedule with assigned tasks keeps you on track but should allow changes for unexpected events.
14. Low motivation days are normal; aim for smaller targets or ask a friend for a little push.
15. Check that your chosen activities are safe for your body, mind, and finances.

Conclusion

Recovery is not only about stopping a harmful habit. It also involves filling your life with tasks that help you feel centered and ready to face daily problems. This chapter provided you with many ideas for mind and body activities—some are very common, like walking or reading, and some may be new to you, like mini science activities or creative movement with objects.

Feel free to mix and match suggestions until you find a set of routines that fits your needs. Over time, you might develop a personal list of favorite tasks that keep your mood steadier and your body healthier. When done regularly, these actions can form a strong barrier against negative urges or thoughts, making the path away from addiction more stable.

In the next chapters, we will build on these foundations, exploring how to handle urges and cravings (Chapter 9) and keep growing your self-worth without relying on the old habit (Chapter 10). By using the mental tools you have gained so far, along with the fresh activities described here, you can keep moving forward in a safer and more assured way.

CHAPTER 9: HANDLING URGES AND CRAVINGS

Introduction
After moving away from a harmful habit, you might notice that the urge to return to it can show up without warning. These urges and cravings can be physical, emotional, or a mix of both. Some days they might feel mild, while on other days they might feel strong enough to distract you from your tasks or push you into risky decisions. The key is to understand what cravings are, why they happen, and how to face them with calm determination.

In this chapter, we will look at practical steps to manage urges before they grow out of control. You will learn how to spot the warning signs, use methods to reduce their intensity, and move on without giving in. We will cover basic ideas, as well as advanced tips for those times when cravings feel overwhelming. The goal is to give you more control over your behavior so you can keep building a healthier life.

9.1 What Are Urges and Cravings?

Urges and **cravings** are strong desires to repeat a past behavior. They can show up as thoughts, bodily sensations, or emotional pushes:

- **Thought-Based**: You might think, "Just once more," or "I need it right now."
- **Physical**: Your mouth might water if it was a substance you used to smoke, drink, or eat. You might feel jittery or tense if it was another habit.
- **Emotional**: A sudden wave of stress, sadness, or excitement can lead to the thought, "I need my old habit to handle this feeling."

These experiences are common and do not mean you have failed. They are signals from the body and mind that they want something familiar. However, you are not a robot. You can learn to observe these signals and choose a different path.

9.2 Why Do They Happen?

Cravings often occur because the brain links certain triggers with the reward of the old behavior. Even though you have chosen to stop, the brain's memory may still hold onto cues:

1. **Learned Pathway**: If you always used a substance or did a habit when feeling stressed, your mind formed a link: "Stress = use that substance." Breaking this link takes time.
2. **Pleasure Chemicals**: Some habits release chemicals in the brain that produce a brief feeling of pleasure or relief. The brain remembers that quick comfort and longs for it.
3. **Old Routines**: Daily patterns—like coming home from work or meeting certain friends—might trigger cravings because that was your usual routine in the past.

Understanding these causes helps you see cravings as a mental or physical process, not a personal weakness.

9.3 Recognizing Early Signs of Cravings

Often, cravings start with small hints before growing strong. If you can catch them early, you have a better chance of handling them:

- **Minor Annoyance or Tension**: You might notice a brief feeling of being on edge.
- **Subtle Thoughts**: A tiny idea pops up, like, "Wouldn't it be nice if I could…"
- **Physical Changes**: Sweaty palms, faster heartbeat, or feeling warm without clear reason.

At this early stage, pausing and naming the sensation can stop it from getting bigger. Say to yourself, "I am noticing the start of an urge," or "I feel the pull to do that again." Identifying it out loud or in your mind can interrupt the cycle.

9.4 Immediate Steps to Control an Oncoming Urge

When an urge hits, there are quick steps you can take:

1. **Pause and Breathe**: Close your eyes for a moment (if it is safe to do so), and take three slow, deep breaths. This basic act can calm the rush of thoughts and slow your heart rate.
2. **Change Location**: If possible, move to a different room or step outside. A sudden change of setting breaks the link in your mind between the urge and the place you are in.
3. **Quick Task**: Pick a simple activity like splashing water on your face, folding a towel, or checking your mailbox. By doing something else for a short moment, you give the craving time to weaken.

These small strategies sound almost too easy, but they can be powerful in stealing the momentum from an urge.

9.5 Using Mental Reminders

Sometimes, simply reminding yourself of the reasons you quit can keep an urge from overpowering you:

- **List of Reasons**: Carry a short list in your pocket or phone that explains why you left the old habit. You might write, "Better health," "Clearer mind," or "Being trustworthy to my family."
- **Review Consequences**: Recall the problems the habit caused. This is not to drown in guilt, but to remember the real damage it did.
- **Think Forward**: Picture how you will feel tomorrow if you give in today. This can highlight the regret or pain that might follow the short "reward."

A strong reminder can balance the craving's pull with a clear sense of purpose.

9.6 Distraction and Replacement Activities

Cravings often last for a limited window of time. If you can safely distract yourself, the urge may pass:

1. **Physical Movement**: A brisk walk, some stretches, or tidying up a corner of your living space can redirect energy.
2. **Short Mind Games**: Work on a puzzle, do a few brain teasers, or even a small craft project if you have supplies nearby.
3. **Creative Outlet**: Sketch, write a few lines in a journal, or experiment with simple music.

These actions give your mind a new focus. They do not fix every issue, but they prevent you from sitting idle while the craving grows.

9.7 Plan for High-Risk Times and Places

Certain moments or places can trigger a stronger craving:

- **End of a Long Day**: Fatigue can lower your guard, making cravings feel stronger.
- **Payday or Extra Cash**: Having unplanned money might tempt you to spend it on harmful items or experiences.
- **Certain Social Events**: Gatherings where others use substances can push you to follow old patterns.

To handle these situations, set up a plan. For instance:

- **Safe Rides**: If you are going to an event where you might be tempted, arrange your own ride so you can leave when you want.
- **Scheduled Activities**: If nights are tough, plan a wind-down routine like a calm bath or a relaxing playlist.
- **Limited Cash**: Keep only a small amount of cash on you if that helps you avoid buying harmful items.

Being proactive can reduce the chance of cravings taking you by surprise.

9.8 Support Systems for Cravings

One powerful way to handle urges is to reach out to others:

- **Phone a Friend**: Have at least one person you can call or text to say, "I am feeling a strong urge right now." A quick chat can lighten the weight of the craving.
- **Online Support**: Join forums or groups where people understand. Posting about your feelings can bring supportive replies and tips.
- **Local Meetings**: Recovery groups often talk about cravings openly. You might learn new methods from people who have faced similar experiences.

Remember, you are not bothering others by speaking up. Genuine friends or group members usually want to be there for you in hard times.

9.9 Surfing the Wave of Cravings (Urge Surfing)

"Urge surfing" is a mental method where you treat the craving like a wave in the ocean:

1. **Notice the Craving**: Understand that it has a rise, peak, and fall, much like a wave.
2. **Observe Sensations**: Instead of fighting the urge directly, observe how it feels in your body. Maybe there is tightness in your chest or a flutter in your stomach.
3. **Stay Curious**: Try not to judge the craving as "good" or "bad." Accept that it is there, and watch as it grows, then eventually fades.

Many people find that by calmly observing and not panicking, the craving loses some of its power. It is still uncomfortable, but it becomes something you can watch until it passes.

9.10 Handling Cravings That Emerge from Emotions

Cravings can be tied to deep feelings like anger, sadness, or even excitement. If you have not learned safe ways to manage these emotions, an urge might come to "fix" them:

- **Identify the Emotion**: Ask yourself, "What am I feeling right now?" Giving it a name—like "sad," "angry," or "lonely"—is the first step.
- **Find a Healthy Release**: For anger, some people punch a pillow or write down their frustrations. For sadness, a gentle cry or a talk with a friend can bring relief.
- **Seek Professional Help**: If certain emotions are too strong or linked to past trauma, speaking with a counselor can provide deeper strategies.

When you learn to face your emotions in a safer way, cravings lose their power as a coping tool.

9.11 Setting Boundaries with People Who Trigger Urges

Sometimes, the biggest triggers are individuals in your life:

- **Old Friends Who Use**: They might say, "Come on, one time won't hurt."
- **Family Who Doubt You**: They may not believe you can stay healthy and could push you into a corner.
- **Romantic Partners in Old Habits**: If a partner still uses a substance or engages in risky habits, it can be tough to resist.

Setting boundaries means deciding what you will and will not allow. For instance, you can say, "I am not comfortable being around use of any substance," or "I need you to respect that I cannot go to those parties." If they refuse to honor these boundaries, you might need to limit time spent with them or step away fully. It is not always easy, but your well-being is a priority.

9.12 Advanced Methods for Stronger Cravings

Sometimes basic steps are not enough. Here are more advanced ways to face powerful urges:

1. **Thought Stopping**: When a craving-related thought pops up, you can say "Stop" (either out loud or in your head). Then replace that thought with a simple statement like, "I am in control."

2. **Visual Cues**: Some people carry a small object (like a coin or smooth stone) to hold when an urge arrives. Focusing on that object can ground your thoughts, similar to a reminder of your recovery.
3. **Planned Reminders**: Set alerts on your phone with messages like, "Remember why you quit," or "You can handle this," scheduled at times you expect cravings.

These methods can give you more tools for moments when the usual strategies seem too weak.

9.13 Handling Slip-Ups or Near Misses

There may be times when you almost give in or you have a small slip. This does not erase all your progress. It is a sign that you need to analyze what happened:

- **Review the Lead-Up**: What was going on before the slip or near miss? Were you stressed, tired, or around unsafe people?
- **Write Down Lessons**: Note which tools you used (or did not use). This is not about blaming yourself; it is about learning for the future.
- **Talk It Out**: Discuss the slip-up with a counselor, friend, or group. Getting an outside view can bring fresh insights.

A slip does not have to become a full return to old ways. It is a chance to strengthen your approach and keep moving forward.

9.14 Rewarding Yourself After Resisting an Urge

It can help to have a small reward system. When you notice a craving and choose not to give in, plan a little positive treat for yourself:

- **Healthy Snacks**: If allowed, enjoy a favorite fruit smoothie or a small dessert.
- **Leisure Time**: Give yourself permission to watch a short funny video or listen to a song you love.
- **Quiet Comfort**: Light a soothing candle, take a warm bath, or sit outside for fresh air.

These rewards might seem small, but they reinforce the idea that staying on track brings good feelings. Over time, this can counter the "quick reward" lie that the old habit promises.

9.15 Less-Known Ideas for Urge Management

Below are some ideas that might not be in basic recovery advice:

1. **Finger Tapping Patterns**: Gently tap your fingers in a sequence (index, middle, ring, pinky) on a surface. Count the taps in your head. This simple focus can give your brain a short break from the urge.
2. **Writing Yourself a Urge Pass**: Create a small card that says, "I give myself permission to wait 15 minutes before doing anything about this urge." Often, the urge weakens in that time.
3. **Observation of Craving Characters**: Imagine your craving is a cartoon character talking nonsense. You listen, but you do not have to obey. This can bring a bit of humor and distance to an otherwise serious feeling.

9.16 Using Technology Wisely

Technology can either help you or make things worse:

- **Helpful Apps**: Some apps track the number of days since you quit, giving little awards or motivational messages. Others offer guided meditations or quick coping exercises.
- **Smart Online Boundaries**: If seeing certain content triggers you, consider blocking those accounts or websites.
- **Text and Call Support**: Create a small group chat with people who cheer each other on or respond to cravings in real time.

Use technology as a tool to stay connected and motivated, but be aware of triggers it can bring if used carelessly.

9.17 Combining All Strategies for Personal Success

Every person's urges have a unique pattern. Some people notice them more in the morning, others at night. Some experience them mostly when alone, while others feel them in social gatherings. The best plan is to combine different strategies:

1. **Keep a Craving Journal**: Write down when urges happen, what caused them, how strong they were, and what helped them pass.
2. **Cycle of Support**: Involve at least one friend or group in your daily or weekly plan.
3. **Regular Self-Care**: Good sleep, reasonable exercise, balanced meals, and emotional outlets all lower overall vulnerability to cravings.

By mixing these methods, you build a defense system that can handle cravings from multiple angles.

9.18 Key Points from Chapter 9

1. Urges and cravings are common signals that may be physical, mental, or emotional.
2. They happen because of learned pathways, pleasure chemicals, and old routines.
3. Early signs include small mood shifts, quick thoughts, or light physical changes.
4. Quick steps like breathing, leaving the room, or doing a short task can stop an urge from building.
5. Mental reminders—why you quit and what the old habit cost you—can restore resolve.
6. Distractions (like movement or puzzles) help you ride out the craving's peak.
7. Planning for risky times (end of day, social events, payday) reduces surprise attacks.
8. Support from friends, groups, or hotlines can be a lifeline during intense cravings.
9. Urge surfing teaches you to watch the craving rise and fall without panicking.

10. Emotions like anger or sadness can spark urges, so learning to handle these feelings in a healthier way is important.
11. Boundaries protect you from people who pressure you to return to unsafe habits.
12. Advanced methods like thought stopping, visual cues, and planned alerts give extra layers of defense.
13. Slip-ups do not erase progress; they offer lessons for future success.
14. Rewarding yourself after resisting an urge can anchor positive behavior in your daily life.
15. Simple tactics like finger tapping, an "urge pass," or cartoon imagery can bring relief.
16. Technology can help you track progress or reach out for support, but watch out for triggers.
17. Combining tools—like a craving journal, social support, and consistent self-care—creates a solid plan for handling urges.

Conclusion

Urges and cravings do not have to control your decisions. By building awareness of what they are, why they happen, and how to respond, you can prevent them from leading you back to risky actions. This chapter explored many methods, from short-term fixes like breathing or leaving a room, to deeper approaches like urge surfing and emotional management.

Each time you face a craving, you reinforce the idea that you have a choice. Over time, these urges often appear less frequently and with less power. Even when they do show up, you will be able to handle them in calmer, safer ways. This skill is a major step toward a more stable, free life.

Next, in Chapter 10, we will talk about building self-worth without harmful habits. Often, people in recovery discover that they need a new sense of personal value. By working on real confidence and self-respect, you will be better protected against future cravings and more able to lead the life you want.

CHAPTER 10: BUILDING SELF-WORTH WITHOUT HARMFUL HABITS

Introduction

Self-worth is more than just feeling good about yourself. It is the deep understanding that you have value and can handle the ups and downs of life. After leaving a harmful habit, many people realize their sense of worth was tied to that behavior or substance—or was hidden under feelings of guilt and shame. Now that you have stepped away from the habit, it is time to rebuild a stronger picture of who you are and what you can achieve.

In this chapter, we will look at what self-worth means and how to grow it without returning to old, damaging patterns. We will explore practical tools such as self-honesty, goal-setting, and daily self-respect actions. You will also learn how to deal with setbacks in a way that does not tear down your sense of value. By understanding and nurturing self-worth, you open the door to a future where you are not always defined by your past struggles.

10.1 Defining Self-Worth

Self-worth means believing you have inherent value as a person. It involves respecting yourself, trusting your abilities, and being okay with your flaws. It is not about being perfect or above everyone else; it is about recognizing that you matter, just like any other human being.

- **Difference from Self-Esteem**: Self-esteem can fluctuate if you fail a task or get negative feedback. Self-worth, on the other hand, runs deeper. It says, "I am valuable simply because I exist, not because I excel at everything."
- **Link to Recovery**: When people do not feel worthy, they might turn to substances or habits to fill that hole. By strengthening your sense of worth, you reduce the likelihood of seeking false comfort from old patterns.

10.2 Letting Go of Shame and Guilt

Shame and guilt can block self-worth:

- **Shame**: A painful feeling of being unworthy or flawed at the core. It often arises from mistakes or past actions.
- **Guilt**: A remorseful feeling for something you did that you believe was wrong.

Some guilt can be helpful if it pushes you to change or apologize. But staying stuck in shame or excessive guilt can damage your self-view. To move forward:

1. **Differentiate the Action from the Person**: Remind yourself, "I did harmful things, but I am capable of growing. My past does not define all of me."
2. **Seek Forgiveness, If Appropriate**: Sometimes, speaking with someone you wronged or writing them a letter can help free you from constant guilt.
3. **Consider Professional Help**: If shame is too overwhelming, talking to a counselor can ease that burden.

10.3 Honest Self-Reflection

Being honest about your strengths, weaknesses, and past actions can be scary. However, honest self-reflection is necessary to grow authentic self-worth:

- **Daily or Weekly Check**: Ask yourself, "What did I do well today? Where did I fall short? What can I learn?"
- **Self-Compassion**: Treat yourself like a friend who is trying to improve. A friend might gently point out errors but also acknowledge your progress.
- **Safe Spaces**: You might share your reflections with a trusted person or write them in a private journal.

Honesty allows you to see your real abilities. It stops you from basing your self-worth on illusions or denial.

10.4 Setting Realistic Goals and Achieving Them

One way to confirm your self-worth is by reaching small targets you set for yourself. This does not mean you only value yourself if you meet goals, but rather that each success can act as proof that you can move forward:

1. **Pick Goals That Fit**: They could be personal (like exercising three times a week), social (like making one supportive phone call per day), or work-related (like finishing a simple project).
2. **Create Simple Steps**: Break big goals into smaller tasks, so you experience success more often.
3. **Track Your Progress**: Keep a notebook or chart to mark your improvements. Seeing how far you have come can be a big lift for self-worth.

10.5 Daily Acts of Self-Respect

Self-worth grows when you consistently treat yourself in a positive way:

- **Mindful Grooming**: Simple acts like taking a bath, brushing your teeth, or dressing in comfortable, clean clothes can remind you that you deserve care.
- **Healthy Eating**: Filling your plate with balanced meals signals to yourself that your body is worth nourishing.
- **Safe Boundaries**: Respecting your time, your rest, and your emotional space is another way to show you matter.

These actions might sound small, but they add up. Each time you honor your needs, you reinforce the idea that you are important.

10.6 Positive Self-Talk

The things you say to yourself can lift you up or tear you down. If you constantly tell yourself you are useless or hopeless, it is hard to maintain self-worth. Instead, work on:

1. **Noticing Negative Patterns**: When a harsh statement comes up ("I am so stupid!"), pause and recognize it.
2. **Rephrasing**: Swap negative labels with realistic, balanced words. For example, "I made a mistake here, but I can find a solution."
3. **Encouraging Phrases**: Speak to yourself with the same tone you would use for a friend in need. You might say, "I trust myself to learn from this" or "I am doing my best in this moment."

Over time, kinder self-talk becomes more natural, strengthening your inner belief that you have worth.

10.7 Learning to Accept Praise and Support

Some people who struggle with self-worth feel uncomfortable when someone praises them or offers help:

- **Old Beliefs**: You might think you do not deserve praise or support, so you reject it.
- **Fear of Disappointment**: Maybe you fear that if you accept praise, you must always live up to it perfectly.
- **Gently Welcome It**: Practice a simple "thank you" when someone compliments you. Let them know you appreciate their kind words or help.

Accepting positive feedback does not make you arrogant. It is part of growing a balanced sense of value.

10.8 Building Skills and Knowledge

Learning something new can expand your view of who you are:

- **Take a Course**: Whether it is cooking, coding, or any topic of interest, gaining new skills can show you that you are capable of growth.
- **Volunteer in a Field of Interest**: Helping others while learning new tasks can reinforce a sense of purpose.
- **Workshops and Community Events**: Participating in local activities can give you fresh insights and a place to practice new abilities.

Your self-worth does not hinge on one skill or knowledge area, but every addition to your skill set can remind you that you have the power to evolve.

10.9 Handling Criticism

When your self-worth is fragile, criticism can feel devastating. However, no one is perfect. Criticism—if delivered fairly—can help you see areas to improve:

1. **Pause Before Reacting**: Take a deep breath. Notice if your immediate response is to become defensive or to sink into shame.
2. **Find Useful Points**: Ask yourself, "Is there any part of this criticism that is valid and can help me grow?"
3. **Discard Harsh Tones**: If the criticism is just hateful or without reason, remind yourself you do not have to accept unkind attacks. Focus on what might be constructive and let go of the rest.

Over time, learning to handle criticism calmly can become a source of strength, showing you that you can listen, decide, and keep your worth intact.

10.10 Dealing with Setbacks without Losing Self-Worth

No matter how well you plan, life will have obstacles. A relapse, a failed job attempt, or a conflict with a friend can shake you. The challenge is to separate the event from your personal value:

- **Label the Event**: "I had a setback," rather than "I am a failure."
- **Look for Lessons**: Even the worst day can teach you something about what to adjust in the future.
- **Get Support**: Talk to someone who understands that a setback does not define you. Hearing them say, "You can still make progress," can restore your perspective.

By handling setbacks in this way, you keep your self-worth safe, even when external things go wrong.

10.11 Connecting with Supportive People

Spending time with people who treat you with respect and kindness helps rebuild a broken sense of self-worth:

- **Friends and Family Who Are Safe**: Choose those who do not constantly tear you down or remind you of your past in a hurtful way.
- **Recovery Communities**: In many support groups, members uplift each other and understand the fight against harmful habits.
- **Mentors or Life Coaches**: A mentor in your field of interest can give you honest feedback and support your growth, which helps confirm your value.

The key is to cultivate circles where you feel accepted, not judged.

10.12 Practicing Gratitude and Perspective

A focus on gratitude can help you see that you matter as part of a bigger picture:

- **Daily Gratitude Note**: Write one or two things you are grateful for, which can include personal traits you are proud of.
- **Shift Your View**: When you do something kind or complete a task, notice how it benefits others, too. Understanding that your actions have positive effects can raise your sense of worth.
- **Share Thankfulness**: Sometimes, just telling someone "Thank you for being supportive" can remind both of you that you are in a caring community.

Gratitude is not about ignoring problems; it is about noticing the good that exists alongside challenges.

10.13 Handling Negative Self-Comparisons

Comparing yourself to others is a sure path to feeling less than or worthless. Remember:

1. **Everyone's Path Is Different**: You might see someone who seems to have it all together, but they could be hiding their own problems.
2. **Compare Self to Past Self**: Look at where you used to be compared to now. Notice the steps you have taken.
3. **Limit Social Media Overuse**: Constant images of success can make you doubt your own worth. Sometimes, stepping back from these feeds is better for your mental health.

You have your own pace, your own strengths, and your own lessons. This uniqueness is part of your value.

10.14 Practical Exercises for Self-Worth

Below are some tasks you can do daily or weekly to reinforce a healthier view of yourself:

1. **Self-Worth Journal**: Write three things you appreciate about yourself. These can be personality traits ("I'm patient"), actions ("I helped my neighbor"), or qualities ("I'm honest").
2. **Mirror Check**: Look in the mirror for a moment and say something supportive to yourself—like, "I am worthy of kindness." It may feel awkward at first, but it helps to challenge old, negative habits.
3. **Skill Spotlight**: Once a week, focus on one skill you are proud of. Reflect on how you developed it and how you can use it more. This reminds you that you can achieve good things.

10.15 Overcoming Fear of Success

Strangely, some people fear success as much as they fear failure. They worry that if they do well, more will be expected of them, or they will have to maintain a higher standard:

- **Small Successes Are Still Successes**: Recognize that even small improvements—like sticking to a healthy routine for a day—are steps forward.

- **Give Yourself Permission to Shine**: Practice saying, "It is okay for me to do well. I can handle what comes next, one step at a time."
- **Check Old Beliefs**: If you were taught that you do not deserve happiness or success, it is time to question and replace that belief.

Building self-worth includes allowing yourself to do well without sabotaging your own progress out of fear.

10.16 Finding Meaning in Your Daily Actions

Your sense of value can also grow when you see that your life has meaning:

- **Serve a Need**: Whether it is helping a local cause or supporting a friend, knowing you have a role that matters boosts your inner sense of worth.
- **Spend Time on What Resonates with You**: If you feel drawn to certain forms of art, nature, or community work, give yourself permission to explore them.
- **Celebrate Diversity**: Notice how your unique background and experiences allow you to contribute something special to the world around you.

Seeing that your existence has a positive impact can lessen doubts about whether you matter.

10.17 Putting Self-Worth into Action

Having self-worth is not just about private feelings. It affects how you behave:

1. **Decision-Making**: When you feel valuable, you make choices that align with your well-being rather than choices driven by fear or self-hate.
2. **Speaking Up**: A person with growing self-worth can speak for their needs or say "no" without shame.
3. **Seeking Growth**: You are more likely to try new hobbies, meet new people, or challenge yourself in safe ways because you trust you can handle things.

These shifts in action can create a cycle—positive behavior supports a stronger sense of worth, which in turn leads to more positive behavior.

10.18 Key Points from Chapter 10

1. Self-worth is the steady belief that you are valuable, beyond your successes or mistakes.
2. Guilt and shame can block self-worth. Learning to separate your actions from your core identity is key to moving forward.
3. Honest self-reflection, including recognizing your strengths and weaknesses, lays the foundation for authentic growth.
4. Small, realistic goals provide evidence that you can follow through and deserve credit for your efforts.
5. Daily acts of self-respect—like basic self-care and healthy boundaries—reinforce the idea that you matter.
6. Positive self-talk counters old messages of worthlessness.
7. Accepting praise or support can be challenging at first, but it is a step toward recognizing your own value.
8. Learning new skills or knowledge is a practical way to prove to yourself that you can make progress.
9. Criticism does not have to destroy your self-view; you can use it to learn without letting it define your worth.
10. Setbacks are events, not reflections of who you are. Seek lessons and remember your value.
11. Surround yourself with people who show respect and kindness; their input can help you see your strengths.
12. Gratitude shifts the focus from what is lacking to what is present and good in your life.
13. Avoid comparing yourself to others. Focus on your own journey and personal improvements.
14. Daily or weekly exercises like writing self-appreciations or looking in the mirror with kindness can support steady growth in self-worth.
15. Fear of success can be as real as fear of failure. Welcome small achievements and allow yourself to advance.
16. Finding meaning in your work, friendships, or interests helps you see the importance of your presence in the world.

17. A strong sense of worth influences your choices and encourages a healthy push for personal growth.

Conclusion

Building self-worth after letting go of a harmful habit is a gradual process. It requires honest reflection, daily practice, and the courage to accept that you are more than your past. Each positive step—whether it is a small goal met, a healthy boundary kept, or a negative thought challenged—adds another layer to your core confidence.

As you continue to strengthen your sense of worth, you will find it easier to resist urges, handle stress, and grow in new directions. This change does not happen overnight, but with steady effort, you can begin to see yourself as a person worthy of respect, both from others and from yourself. In the upcoming chapters, we will explore communication tips, problem-solving skills, and other tools to help you keep building on this foundation of self-worth. By combining a healthy view of yourself with practical life skills, you give yourself the best chance at a safer, stronger future.

CHAPTER 11: COMMUNICATING IN A NEW WAY

Introduction
Communication goes beyond just talking. It involves listening, noticing nonverbal signals, choosing the right words, and showing respect to both yourself and the person you are speaking with. After dealing with a harmful habit, you might find that your communication style changed during the tough periods. Perhaps you spoke harshly due to stress, avoided important conversations, or hid behind untrue statements to cover your actions. Now that you are on a safer path, it is time to learn or improve methods that help you connect openly with others.

This chapter will explain different approaches to express yourself clearly, handle disagreements calmly, and respond to people in a way that respects their perspective while still honoring your own needs. By adding these methods to your daily life, you can bring fresh stability to your relationships. Whether you are communicating with family members, co-workers, friends, or even strangers, these ideas can help you feel more confident and less tense.

11.1 Understanding What Healthy Communication Looks Like

Healthy communication has several key features:

1. **Honesty**: You speak truthfully while respecting the other person's feelings.
2. **Active Listening**: You focus on what the other person is saying, rather than just planning your response.
3. **Respectful Tone**: You avoid name-calling, shouting, or threatening language, even during disagreements.
4. **Clarity**: You say what you mean using words that match your real thoughts, reducing confusion and misunderstandings.

It is normal not to get it all right every single time. The goal is to work on making your exchanges with others more open and less harmful.

11.2 Letting Go of Old Patterns

In the past, you may have had moments of defensive communication—fearing blame or judgment—or you might have told partial truths to protect your habit. You might have avoided certain talks altogether, hoping the problem would vanish. Letting go of these habits can be challenging, but once you do:

- **You Build More Trust**: People sense your sincerity when you speak and listen with honesty.
- **You Gain Self-Respect**: Knowing that you are not hiding or twisting words can make you feel more at peace inside.
- **You Reduce Conflict**: Clear, calm discussion prevents arguments from blowing up.

One of the best ways to step out of old patterns is to pay attention to your words and your body cues while speaking. Notice if your heart rate speeds up or if your fists clench, and pause to calm yourself before continuing.

11.3 The Importance of Active Listening

Active listening is a strong tool for better communication. Instead of just hearing words, you focus on the speaker's message with the intent to understand. Key elements of active listening include:

1. **Eye Contact (as culturally appropriate)**: When you look at someone (or at least turn your body toward them if direct eye contact is not comfortable for cultural reasons), you show you are involved.
2. **No Interrupting**: Let them finish their sentences before you speak.
3. **Reflective Statements**: After they talk, you can paraphrase: "So you feel upset because _____?" This helps confirm you got the main point.
4. **Short Affirmations**: Simple words like "I see," "Yes," or "I understand" can keep the flow going without cutting them off.

You might be surprised how much tension can drop when a person feels truly heard. It also gives them a chance to clarify their views if you misunderstood.

11.4 Simple Ways to Express Your Feelings

Sharing your emotions in a safe way can prevent them from building up inside. Instead of lashing out, try:

1. **Use "I" Statements**: Instead of saying, "You never listen to me," say, "I feel unheard when I speak and don't get a reply." This approach reduces blame and invites problem-solving.
2. **Describe, Don't Accuse**: If someone's action upset you, explain what they did and how it made you feel. For instance, "When you left without saying anything, I felt worried." This is more constructive than, "You're so inconsiderate."
3. **Focus on the Present Situation**: Bringing up every past mistake can confuse the current discussion. Stick to the issue at hand.

You do not have to be perfect at this. Even making an effort shows that you are trying to communicate more fairly and respectfully.

11.5 Setting Up Boundaries Through Words

A boundary is a line that keeps your mental and emotional space safe. Communicating these limits with others can help you prevent stress:

- **State Boundaries Clearly**: "I'm not comfortable with yelling. If we raise our voices, I'll take a break."
- **Explain Why They Matter**: "It makes me feel unsafe when voices get too loud, so I need this boundary to stay calm."
- **Enforce the Boundary**: If it is crossed (e.g., someone starts yelling), follow through by leaving the room or ending the conversation politely.

Boundaries help you remain true to your new healthier direction while letting others know that you value respectful and calm interaction.

11.6 Building Assertiveness Without Aggression

Assertiveness sits between the extremes of being passive (never stating your needs) and being aggressive (forcing your needs onto others). Being assertive means standing up for yourself while still respecting others. Consider:

- **Calm Tone**: Even if you feel strongly, do not shout. Speak firmly but evenly.
- **Use Polite Language**: "I would like," "I need," or "I prefer" are clearer than "You must" or "You better."
- **Offer Options**: When possible, suggest a compromise that respects both sides. For example, "I can meet you halfway on this issue by agreeing to your plan some days if you are willing to consider my plan on others."

Practicing assertiveness can feel uneasy at first, but over time it becomes easier and fosters healthier relationships.

11.7 Dealing with Criticism or Harsh Words

No matter how politely you approach a conversation, some people might respond with criticism or blame. Here's how you can handle it:

1. **Pause Before Reacting**: Take a breath or a short silence. This keeps you from replying in anger.
2. **Check for Useful Points**: Is there any truth in what they are saying that might help you improve? If so, acknowledge it.
3. **Stand Firm Against Misuse**: If the words are purely meant to hurt or belittle, calmly state that you do not accept mistreatment. You might say, "I understand you are upset, but I can't continue if we can't keep a respectful tone."
4. **Seek Resolution**: If they calm down, try to find a path forward. If they remain hostile, you might end the conversation until a safer time.

11.8 Supporting Others Through Better Communication

Just as you benefit from healthier communication, people around you do too. Simple acts like:

- **Asking Questions**: Show genuine interest in someone's day or feelings.
- **Offering Encouraging Words**: Say, "I hear what you're saying," or "It seems like this is really important to you."

- **Giving Quiet Time**: If someone is emotional, maybe they need a few moments before talking again. You can say, "I can see this is painful. Let me know when you feel ready to continue."

By being a better listener and a kinder speaker, you set a positive standard for those around you, which can strengthen the bond you share.

11.9 Handling Group Conversations

Group settings can be more complex because more people are speaking. Here are some tips:

- **Stay Aware of Time**: If the group is large, keep your comments clear and short so others have a chance to talk too.
- **Look for Nonverbal Signals**: Does someone look uneasy but hasn't spoken? You might gently invite them: "Did you want to say something?"
- **Avoid Side Talks**: Whispering with one person in a group can cause confusion or make others feel left out.
- **Agree on Rules**: In a formal group or support meeting, it helps to have guidelines like "No interrupting" or "Keep voice volume calm."

Group conversations can be rewarding if everyone practices respectful turn-taking and listening.

11.10 Healing Broken Communication with Family

Families might have years of unresolved tension or misunderstandings. Fixing communication with them can be a big step in your new, healthier life. Try:

1. **Start Small**: Begin with short conversations on neutral topics before tackling big, sensitive ones.
2. **Find a Mediator**: Sometimes a counselor, elder, or neutral friend can help keep the talk constructive.
3. **Admit Past Mistakes**: If your old habit caused lying or withdrawal, acknowledging that damage can open the door to rebuilding trust.

4. **Agree on New Norms**: For instance, decide that from now on, you will not call each other names or bring up past issues unfairly.

It takes time for family wounds to mend, but clearer communication can be a strong first step.

11.11 Electronic Communication: Texts, Emails, and Social Media

Many conversations now happen online or through messaging. While this can be fast and convenient, it can also lead to misunderstandings:

- **Tone Can Be Misread**: What sounds okay in your head might come across as rude when the other person reads it.
- **Keep It Brief**: If it is an emotional topic, it is often better to speak by phone or in person, if possible. Long, heated text exchanges can make problems worse.
- **Wait Before Hitting Send**: If you are upset, save a draft and read it later before sending. This small pause can stop a message that might do harm.
- **Public vs. Private**: Avoid publicly posting angry replies. If you have a conflict, handle it in a private message or face to face.

Electronic chats can help you stay in touch, but remain mindful of how easily things can be misunderstood in written form.

11.12 Getting Help Through Communication Training

If you find that you keep falling into bad habits, you might benefit from professional guidance:

- **Counseling Sessions**: A therapist can teach you specific methods to handle anger or fear in discussions.
- **Workshops or Classes**: Some community centers offer basic communication or conflict-resolution classes.
- **Support Groups**: Regular group meetings can help you practice open communication in a structured environment.

Learning new habits is a process. Seeking training does not mean you are failing—it means you care about doing better.

11.13 Apologizing and Forgiving

When communication leads to hurt, apologies and forgiveness can be part of the healing process:

1. **Sincere Apology**: A real apology takes ownership. Say, "I'm sorry I did that," or "I realize I hurt you. Please help me understand how I can fix it." Avoid putting blame on the other person in your apology.
2. **Avoid Making Excuses**: Resist statements like, "I'm sorry, but you made me angry." That negates the sincerity.
3. **Offer to Make Amends**: Ask, "Is there anything I can do to help you feel better?"
4. **Consider Forgiving**: Forgiveness does not mean denying the hurt; it means you choose not to let the anger control you anymore. Still, forgiving does not require remaining in an unsafe situation. You can forgive in your heart but also set boundaries if needed.

11.14 Less-Known Communication Tips

Below are a few tips that might not show up in typical advice guides:

1. **Communicate in Writing if Speech Feels Overwhelming**: If strong emotions prevent a calm talk, writing a letter (even if you do not send it) can help you organize your thoughts. Then, if you do share it, the other person has time to process your words.
2. **Use a Timer for Each Person**: In heated situations, you can agree that each person gets two minutes to speak without interruption, and then the other responds. It might feel odd, but it ensures fairness.
3. **'Focus Object' in Group Discussion**: If you are in a small group, pass around a small item (like a stress ball). Only the person holding it can speak, and then they pass it on. This prevents interruptions and signals everyone's turn to share.

11.15 Building Self-Awareness for Better Communication

Your communication improves when you notice your own triggers and emotional states:

- **Track Emotional Swings**: If you are more irritated when hungry or tired, watch out for those times and attempt calmer approaches or wait to discuss big matters.
- **Learn to Pause**: If you sense you are getting upset, say something like, "I need a moment," and step away to breathe or drink water.
- **Reflect After Talks**: Ask yourself: "What went well? What did not?" Over time, you will see patterns and can practice better responses.

Self-awareness can prevent explosive arguments and help you grow as a stronger communicator.

11.16 Communication When You Feel Vulnerable

Some conversations might bring up deep fears or past shame:

- **Pick a Good Setting**: Choose a quiet place where you feel safe.
- **Speak Slowly**: Do not rush your words. If you feel shaky, it is okay to pause and gather your thoughts.
- **Have a Support Person Nearby**: If it is a really delicate topic (like past trauma), you might want a counselor or trusted friend present.

Being open about your vulnerabilities can be scary, but in the right context, it can lead to deeper understanding and strong, respectful bonds.

11.17 Handling Communication with Children

If you have children, your communication style affects how they learn to express themselves:

1. **Be Clear and Consistent**: Explain rules and consequences calmly, and follow through if a limit is broken.

2. **Encourage Their Thoughts**: Ask for their opinions and ideas, even if they are small. This builds their self-esteem.
3. **Avoid Name-Calling or Shaming**: Correct their behavior, but do not tear down their identity. For example, say, "That was not the right choice," instead of, "You're a bad kid."
4. **Listen to Their Feelings**: Even if their complaints seem minor, let them know you hear them. They will learn that calm expression of feelings is okay.

Children who experience patient and clear communication often develop fewer issues with anger or secrecy as they grow.

11.18 Key Points from Chapter 11

1. Healthy communication includes honesty, active listening, and clarity.
2. Letting go of old patterns like hiding truths or avoiding talks can greatly reduce conflict and build trust.
3. Active listening involves giving full attention and reflecting back what the speaker says.
4. Sharing feelings with "I" statements stops blame and invites collaboration.
5. Boundaries let you protect your emotional well-being during talks or disagreements.
6. Being assertive means stating your needs with respect, not aggression.
7. Criticism can be considered calmly, picking out useful bits while rejecting disrespect.
8. Group talks require clear time-sharing, awareness of others' signals, and agreed-upon rules.
9. Healing family communication may need professional help or structured discussions.
10. Online chats need careful tone management; a short pause before sending a message can prevent trouble.
11. Apologies and forgiveness have the power to repair hurt, but they need to be genuine.
12. Less-known tips like writing letters or using timers can keep communication from spinning out of control.
13. Self-awareness of your triggers and emotional states can help you handle tough moments better.

14. Conversations about vulnerable topics should happen in a safe place, possibly with a support person.
15. Communicating with children involves consistency, patience, and focus on their thoughts and feelings.

Conclusion

Learning to speak and listen in a clear, respectful way helps you maintain healthy relationships and safeguard your mental well-being. It also allows you to express yourself without building guilt or shame. Whether in one-on-one talks, family settings, or group discussions, effective communication reduces stress and increases trust. If you find yourself struggling, remember that help is available—through counselors, support groups, or classes. By improving how you speak and listen, you affirm your new, healthier life and build bonds that can keep you moving in a better direction.

In the next chapter, you will discover methods to solve day-to-day problems in a structured way. These approaches, combined with good communication, will help you prevent small bumps from growing into major obstacles on your path to lasting health.

CHAPTER 12: PROBLEM-SOLVING METHODS FOR EVERYDAY LIFE

Introduction

Life is made up of both small and large problems. Some are routine, like not having enough time to do chores, while others are more urgent, like facing a financial crisis or dealing with a sudden conflict at work. In the past, you might have turned to harmful habits as a way to handle stress or run away from problems. But now, with a clearer mind and stronger focus on health, you have the chance to learn new problem-solving skills that can keep stress from piling up.

In this chapter, you will gain practical steps to address everyday challenges, from organizing finances to settling disagreements with friends. You will see how to break problems down into steps, brainstorm answers, pick the best solution, and review how it all turned out. By practicing these methods, you show yourself that you can handle the unexpected with less fear and more stability.

12.1 Why Problem-Solving Skills Matter

Strong problem-solving skills can improve your mental health in several ways:

1. **Lower Stress**: When you have a plan, worries lose some of their power.
2. **Better Confidence**: Success with small tasks gives you proof that you can manage bigger ones.
3. **Less Risk of Relapse**: If you have a method for dealing with challenges, you are less likely to seek temporary escape in old habits.

Problems will always show up in life. But how you approach them can be the difference between feeling trapped and feeling in control.

12.2 Recognizing the Real Problem

Sometimes, the main issue is hidden under smaller complaints or emotional reactions. For instance:

- **Surface Complaint**: "I hate my job."
- **Actual Problem**: You might feel unsafe around a co-worker or lack clear direction from a boss.
- **Another Surface Complaint**: "I'm always late on my bills."
- **Actual Problem**: Maybe you do not have a budget, or you are unemployed, or you have too many unnecessary expenses.

To tackle any challenge effectively, you must define it clearly. Ask yourself, "What exactly is wrong here?" and "Is there a root issue I need to solve before everything else?"

12.3 Step-by-Step Method for Basic Problem-Solving

A simple model for problem-solving follows these steps:

1. **Identify the Problem**: Write it out briefly.
2. **Brainstorm Solutions**: List any idea that comes to mind, even if it seems far-fetched.
3. **Weigh the Pros and Cons**: Look at the good and bad sides of each idea.
4. **Pick One**: Choose the solution that looks most reasonable and doable.
5. **Plan and Act**: Break your chosen solution into small tasks and carry them out.
6. **Review the Results**: Did it fix the problem? If not, try another idea or adjust your plan.

Doing these steps on paper can make it feel more structured and less overwhelming.

12.4 Brainstorming Without Judgment

Brainstorming means letting your mind generate as many answers as possible before judging them. Tips for brainstorming:

1. **Write Everything Down**: Even a "bad" idea can spark a better one.
2. **Stay Open**: If you are stuck, imagine you are giving advice to a friend. Sometimes, you will see fresh options.

3. **Use Past Success**: Recall times you solved similar issues. Could those methods help here?

Once you have a list of possible fixes, you can examine them logically.

12.5 Practical Tools for Organizing Solutions

If you struggle with juggling many responsibilities, try:

- **To-Do Lists**: Write down tasks each day in order of importance. Cross them off as you complete them.
- **Calendars and Reminders**: A physical planner or a phone app can keep track of deadlines.
- **Priority Grid**: List tasks in four boxes: urgent and important, urgent but less important, important but not urgent, and neither. Focus on the top boxes first.

Organizing your approach reduces the chance of forgetting crucial tasks or feeling lost.

12.6 Breaking Down Big Problems

Large issues—like finding a new job or moving to a new place—can seem overwhelming. Breaking them down can help:

1. **Name the Main Goal**: For example, "I need a stable job that pays my bills."
2. **Split Into Sub-Goals**: "Rewrite my resume, search online for job openings, apply to three positions a week, prepare for interviews."
3. **Set Timelines**: "By the end of this week, I will update my resume."
4. **Reward Small Wins**: After submitting your applications, do something small and nice for yourself—like reading a chapter of a fun book or chatting with a friend.

When you see steady progress, the big challenge does not look as scary.

12.7 Handling Emotional Stress During Problem-Solving

Difficult situations can cause anxiety, anger, or sadness, which might cloud your thinking. To keep clarity:

1. **Pause for Breathing**: Before you jump into solutions, take a few slow, deep breaths. This can calm racing thoughts.
2. **Share Feelings with Someone Trustworthy**: Talking out your worries can lighten the mental load.
3. **Use a Journal**: Write about your emotions, then switch to listing possible solutions. This creates a boundary between feeling upset and taking action.

Balancing your emotions with practical steps allows you to handle the process without being paralyzed by fear or frustration.

12.8 Collaborative Problem-Solving

Sometimes, a problem affects not just you but also family members, roommates, or co-workers. In these cases:

- **Call a Meeting**: Set a time to talk about the issue calmly.
- **Use "We" Language**: "How can we solve this?" instead of "You need to fix this."
- **Combine Brainstorm Lists**: Everyone lists solutions, then you all weigh pros and cons together.
- **Agree on Roles**: Who does what? By when? Write down tasks so each person is clear on their part.

When people feel included in the process, they are more likely to stick to the plan and less likely to blame each other.

12.9 Dealing with Setbacks and Plan B

Not every solution will work perfectly on the first try:

1. **Accept the Possibility of Failure**: That does not mean you give up; it means you plan for it.
2. **Track Early Warning Signs**: If something is not working, can you adjust parts of the solution right away?
3. **Prepare a Secondary Option**: Have a plan B if your first solution fails. This can keep you from feeling hopeless when faced with unexpected obstacles.

Learning to bounce back is a major part of effective problem-solving. It also helps you trust your resilience.

12.10 Finding Outside Resources

Some problems require professional help or resources you do not have personally:

- **Financial Advice**: Free counseling sessions at local non-profit groups can show you how to budget or manage debt.
- **Legal Matters**: If you face a legal issue, find an organization that offers advice or representation at low cost.
- **Job Training**: Government programs sometimes provide free or discounted courses to improve your skills.
- **Emotional Support**: A therapist or support group can be crucial if the problem involves mental health or complex relationship dynamics.

Do not let pride stop you from seeking help. Using available resources is part of being a strong problem-solver, not a sign of weakness.

12.11 Time Management for Problem-Solving

You might have many tasks at once—chores, job tasks, family duties—so you need to carve out time to solve new problems:

1. **Set Specific "Problem-Solving Blocks"**: Choose certain hours or days to focus on an ongoing issue, so you do not push it aside indefinitely.

2. **Delegate Where Possible**: If you have supportive friends or family, assign them tasks. This frees you to focus on what only you can do.
3. **Avoid Overloading One Day**: Spread tasks out through the week. Tackling too many problems at once can drain your energy and clarity.

Good time management prevents emergencies by handling issues early, before they spiral out of control.

12.12 Mental Tricks for Finding Fresh Ideas

Sometimes, no matter how much you think, the answers are not clear. Here are some mental tricks to find solutions you might not see at first:

- **Take a Different View**: Ask yourself, "If I were 10 years older, how would I see this problem?" or "If I had a mentor, what would they suggest?"
- **Mind Map**: Write the problem in the center of a paper, draw branches for major factors or possible fixes, and keep branching out details.
- **Change the Setting**: Try thinking about the problem in a park, a cafe, or a library. A new environment can spark new ideas.

These methods can break you out of a mental rut and open up options you did not consider earlier.

12.13 Staying Motivated Through the Process

Keeping motivation high is crucial, especially when the road to a solution is long:

1. **Focus on the Benefits**: Remind yourself why solving this problem matters. Maybe it will bring peace, financial stability, or stronger relationships.
2. **Track Small Successes**: Each time you complete a sub-goal, note it in a journal or on a calendar.
3. **Use Positive Self-Talk**: Tell yourself, "I'm making progress," or "I can handle this step." Even if it feels forced at first, these messages can push you to keep going.

Motivation can ebb and flow, so plan for days when you feel tired by breaking tasks into smaller bites. A bit of progress is better than none.

12.14 Handling Conflicts as Part of Problem-Solving

Some problems involve direct conflict with people—maybe you disagree with your partner about finances or have a quarrel with a neighbor about noise. In these cases:

- **Stay on the Main Topic**: Do not shift into personal attacks or bring up old grudges. Focus on solving the immediate issue, like "We need to agree on a household budget."
- **Offer Neutral Meeting Places**: If possible, pick a calm location to talk, such as a local library's meeting room or a quiet cafe.
- **Seek a Mediator**: If you keep arguing without progress, look for someone neutral who can guide the discussion. This could be a counselor, community leader, or a friend both parties trust.

When handled calmly, conflicts can lead to healthier agreements and a sense of relief once resolved.

12.15 Unexpected Problems and Crisis Management

Life can throw sudden crises at you: a car breakdown, a sudden injury, or a friend in emergency need. Some tips for these urgent cases:

1. **Stay Calm**: Take one or two deep breaths to steady your mind before you act.
2. **Evaluate Immediate Needs**: Is anyone in danger? Address safety first—call emergency services if needed.
3. **Gather Facts**: What exactly happened? Who is affected? What resources do you have right now?
4. **Take Quick Action**: If you know a partial fix, do it. For instance, if your car is stuck, call for roadside help right away rather than panicking.
5. **Ask for Support**: In a crisis, do not hesitate to contact friends, relatives, or professional services.

After the immediate crisis passes, review what you learned to handle future emergencies more efficiently.

12.16 Less-Known Problem-Solving Tips

Below are a few methods that are not always mentioned in typical advice:

1. **"Worst-Case to Best-Case" Technique**: Write out the worst-case scenario, the best-case scenario, and the likely middle ground. This can calm extreme worry by showing you that the actual outcome is often somewhere in between.
2. **Use a Buddy System**: Pair up with a friend who is also working through problems. Check in daily or weekly and talk about what steps you took. Mutual accountability can boost motivation.
3. **Visualization**: Picture yourself successfully handling the problem. This is not magical thinking; it is a mental practice that can lower anxiety and sharpen focus.

12.17 Reviewing the Results and Adjusting

Once you have attempted a solution, take time to see if it worked:

- **Set a Date to Check Progress**: Maybe one week or a month later, look at where you stand.
- **Ask: "Did I Solve the Core Issue?"**: If yes, note which steps worked well. If not, pinpoint where you got stuck.
- **Fine-Tune**: Make changes to your plan or try a different solution if the first one did not produce the results you hoped for.
- **Celebrate Success Safely**: It is good to acknowledge when you solve a problem. Give yourself credit in a healthy way. For instance, treat yourself to a relaxing activity that fits your new, safer lifestyle (a quiet walk, a favorite book, or time with a positive friend).

12.18 Key Points from Chapter 12

1. Strong problem-solving skills help you face daily challenges and reduce stress, improving overall mental well-being.

2. Clearly define the problem to avoid chasing surface complaints instead of the root cause.
3. A basic six-step model—identify, brainstorm, weigh options, pick one, act, review—offers a structured path to solutions.
4. Brainstorming works best when you temporarily set aside judgment.
5. Tools like to-do lists, calendars, and priority grids keep you organized and prevent overwhelm.
6. Large problems become easier when split into smaller tasks with set timelines.
7. Emotional stress can derail the process, so pause and calm yourself before tackling tasks.
8. Collaborative problem-solving invites everyone to contribute and divides responsibilities fairly.
9. Plan B is part of realistic problem-solving—if your first attempt fails, stay flexible.
10. Use outside resources like financial advisors or counselors if the problem is beyond your knowledge or ability.
11. Good time management ensures you do not neglect important tasks.
12. Mental tricks such as changing your viewpoint or mind-mapping can open new answers.
13. Motivation may dip during long processes; track small wins and speak encouraging words to keep going.
14. Conflicts require calm talks focusing on the issue, possibly with a neutral mediator.
15. Sudden crises call for calm, immediate action, checking who can help, and a quick fix if possible.
16. Less-known tips like using "worst-case to best-case" or pairing with a buddy can boost your success rate.
17. Reviewing and adjusting solutions is essential; a problem-solving plan may need fine-tuning after real-world testing.

Conclusion

Everyday life will always present challenges—missing payments, disagreements at home, unexpected accidents, or any number of stressors. By practicing a structured approach to problem-solving, you build a sense of control and reduce the likelihood of feeling overwhelmed or tempted to return to old, harmful behaviors. Whether you use a simple checklist or seek professional input for bigger issues, you prove to yourself that you can deal with tough situations.

Together with clear communication skills (Chapter 11) and the personal growth methods from earlier chapters, you now have more ways to address problems in a direct, healthy manner. In the next chapters, we will look at how to handle balancing different parts of your life and how to find meaning even in uncertain times. By growing all these skills—communication, problem-solving, self-worth, and more—you strengthen your path to a safer and more fulfilling life.

CHAPTER 13: BALANCING WORK, HOME, AND FREE TIME

Introduction
Once you have a better handle on managing emotional stress, communicating clearly, and solving problems step by step, the next challenge often involves striking a balance among work, home life, and personal free time. Many people feel pulled in different directions, trying to meet demands at their job or school, care for loved ones, and still find a moment of peace for themselves. After dealing with harmful habits, juggling all these areas might seem extra daunting. However, finding a way to keep these parts of life in harmony can lower stress, protect your recovery, and improve overall well-being.

In this chapter, you will learn methods to organize your day, set limits at work and at home, and plan personal moments that help you recharge. We will discuss practical tools such as time-blocking, task prioritization, and healthy downtime ideas. By becoming more deliberate about how you use your hours, you can keep yourself from feeling overloaded, reduce the temptation to rely on old coping habits, and build a more stable lifestyle.

13.1 Why Balancing Life Areas Is So Important

When one area of life takes too much time or energy, you risk burnout, high tension, or weaker relationships. Consider these reasons why balance is worth pursuing:

1. **Mental and Emotional Health**: Excessive work or family pressure can ramp up worry, making it harder to stay calm or avoid cravings.
2. **Physical Well-Being**: When you lack free time, activities that nurture your body—like exercise, cooking a simple healthy meal, or getting enough rest—can slip away.
3. **Better Relationships**: Devoting time to friends and family helps strengthen bonds and foster understanding.
4. **Self-Development**: Having some leisure hours allows you to read, explore new hobbies, or simply reflect on personal goals.

Finding balance is not about perfection. It is about distributing your energy so that each area gets enough attention without overshadowing the others.

13.2 Identifying Your Primary Roles and Responsibilities

Start by listing all the roles you hold. For instance: worker (or student), parent, partner, friend, caretaker of your home, and so on. Next, note your key duties within each role:

- **Work/School**: Tasks, deadlines, projects, or classes.
- **Home**: Cleaning, cooking, organizing bills, childcare, pet care.
- **Self-Care**: Exercise, mindfulness practice, hobbies, medical appointments.
- **Social/Family**: Visiting relatives, staying in touch with friends, celebrating birthdays, or helping others in need.

Seeing all your roles on paper helps you realize the broad scope of your daily life. This clarity can guide you in deciding how to allocate your time more intentionally.

13.3 Setting Realistic Limits and Expectations

Many people experience burnout because they try to do everything at once. Learning to set realistic expectations can protect your mental health:

1. **Avoid Overbooking**: If you take on extra tasks—like volunteering for every event or saying "yes" to every social request—you might leave yourself no time to rest.
2. **Communicate Needs**: If your boss or colleagues keep asking you to work overtime, be honest about your limits if possible. Use calm language, like, "I want to do quality work, but I also need to ensure I have enough time to be at my best."
3. **Reject Perfection**: Doing your best matters more than making everything flawless. Accept that some tasks might be "good enough" instead of perfect.

Learning to say "no" or "I can't right now" is often one of the biggest challenges. Yet it is crucial for staying balanced.

13.4 Time-Blocking and Task Planning

A practical tool for balancing different areas of life is time-blocking, where you schedule specific blocks of time for certain tasks or roles:

- **Create a Daily or Weekly Grid**: Write down hours of the day, from morning to evening. Assign each block to a key role or task. For instance, 8–9 a.m. might be for exercise, 9–12 for work tasks, 12–1 for a lunch break or a quick household errand, etc.
- **Set Start and End Times**: Especially for work or chores, try to define an endpoint. Otherwise, tasks can bleed into the evening and take away free time.
- **Add in Buffers**: Life is unpredictable. Leave small gaps between blocks for short breaks, to handle unexpected calls, or to transition smoothly.

By visually seeing your day, you are less likely to forget important duties or pack in too many tasks. It also helps you notice if there is space for downtime or if you are overscheduling yourself.

13.5 Delegating Tasks at Home and at Work

You do not have to handle all responsibilities alone. Delegation means sharing tasks with others who can help:

- **At Work**: If you have co-workers or a team, see if tasks can be shared based on strengths. For example, you might be better at presentations, while a colleague excels at data analysis.
- **At Home**: Ask family members or roommates to take on some chores. Children can do age-appropriate tasks like folding laundry, setting the table, or watering plants.
- **Barter System**: If you live alone, consider trading tasks with friends or neighbors—for example, you might cook a meal for them if they help you fix a leaky faucet.

Delegating is not shirking responsibility; it is a practical approach that respects your own limits and acknowledges that others can pitch in.

13.6 Balancing Work Pressure with Personal Boundaries

Work can become a significant source of stress if you let job demands spill over into your personal time every day:

1. **Set Clear Hours**: If possible, avoid checking work emails or messages after a certain time in the evening. Some workplaces may expect constant availability, but do your best to define a period to switch off.
2. **Take Breaks Seriously**: During the workday, stand up and stretch, drink water, or go outside for five minutes. Small breaks can rejuvenate your mind and prevent burnout.
3. **Limit Shallow Tasks**: Watch out for draining activities like pointless meetings or online browsing that eat up your focus. Try to group necessary but simpler tasks together and tackle them efficiently.

When you guard your personal boundaries, you are less likely to feel overwhelmed and more able to engage with family or friends at the end of the day.

13.7 Practical Tips for a Less Chaotic Home Life

A chaotic home environment can raise your tension. Luckily, small changes can bring more order:

- **Set Up Routines**: Having a morning routine (waking up, a quick stretch, breakfast, then a short review of the day's to-do list) can ground you.
- **Shared Calendar**: If you live with others, keep a common calendar on the fridge or use a shared app to note everyone's schedules—work shifts, appointments, grocery days, etc.
- **Meal Planning**: Planning meals a few days in advance prevents last-minute food stress. You can cook extra and store leftovers for days when you are busier.
- **Tidy Up Regularly**: Spending 10 minutes tidying each evening can stop chores from piling up and let you wake up to a calmer home.

A more orderly home can reduce mental clutter and free you to focus on other key areas of life.

13.8 Scheduling Free Time and Leisure

Free time is not a luxury; it is a necessary part of self-care and recovery. If you do not schedule it, it might never happen. Ways to protect your leisure:

1. **Short Daily Breaks**: Even 15 minutes of reading, walking, or simply sitting quietly can recharge you.
2. **Weekly Leisure Block**: Set aside a block on weekends or a day off for hobbies, social outings, or just unwinding.
3. **Unplugging**: During your leisure period, consider switching off notifications. Constant pings can rob you of the rest you need.
4. **Micro-Rewards**: After finishing a challenging work task or big household job, reward yourself with a short, enjoyable activity—like listening to a favorite song or phoning a friend.

Protect your break times just as you would protect a vital appointment. This helps keep your energy balanced and your mind calmer.

13.9 Handling Feelings of Guilt When Taking Breaks

Many people feel guilty relaxing, as if every spare minute should be spent on more "productive" tasks. However, rest is productive in its own way:

- **Remind Yourself of the Benefits**: Breaks help prevent burnout and can improve your performance when you return to tasks.
- **Keep It Proportional**: If you have important duties, plan a short or moderate break. There is a difference between a healthy pause and ignoring responsibilities.
- **Remember Your Recovery**: Part of staying safe after a harmful habit is learning healthier ways to cope with stress, including rest.

Try to replace guilt with an understanding that balanced downtime is a vital aspect of mental and physical health, not an indulgence.

13.10 Balancing Social Activities

You might want to spend time with friends and family but also protect your routine and energy:

- **Plan Meetups in Advance**: Spontaneous invites can be fun, but if you tend to overcommit, scheduling gatherings can help you avoid last-minute conflicts.
- **Combine Social and Health Goals**: If you like to exercise, invite a friend to join a short walk. This way, you handle two goals—social bonding and physical activity—at once.
- **Respect Your Budget**: If you are invited to expensive outings frequently, suggest cheaper alternatives like potluck dinners or free local events. Overextending financially can lead to stress and trigger old coping urges.

Social time should enhance your life, not leave you drained or anxious.

13.11 Being Present with Family and Loved Ones

When you finally find a moment for family or close friends, it is easy to let your thoughts drift to unfinished work tasks or daily problems. Being fully present can strengthen those bonds:

1. **Switch Off Devices**: Put your phone on silent or airplane mode for a set period. Give your loved ones your full attention.
2. **Engage in Shared Activities**: Play a short board game, cook together, or watch a light-hearted movie. Doing something side-by-side often leads to deeper connection than just sitting around.
3. **Active Listening**: Ask them about their day. Show genuine interest and provide feedback. This small act can make them feel valued.

When you feel connected at home, it can also lower stress in other areas of your life.

13.12 Avoiding the Trap of "All Work or All Rest"

Some people swing between extremes: working non-stop for days, then crashing and doing nothing for a long stretch. A balanced approach prevents these swings:

- **Aim for Steady Routines**: Even on weekends or days off, try not to sleep way beyond your usual time or skip basic tasks. A little structure maintains a smoother rhythm for your mind and body.
- **Plan Mid-Range Breaks**: Instead of working yourself to exhaustion, schedule moderate breaks regularly. This avoids the cycle of collapse and binge rest.
- **Check Your Energy Levels**: Notice if you are feeling mentally or physically drained. Adjust your routine early rather than pushing until burnout forces you to stop.

Consistency is a friend to long-term recovery and well-being, helping you avoid harmful extremes.

13.13 Handling Unexpected Demands

No matter how well you plan, life can throw surprises—like sudden overtime at work, a family emergency, or an unplanned repair at home. Here is how to adapt:

1. **Prioritize Urgency**: If it is a true emergency, handle it. Shift less urgent tasks to another time.
2. **Re-Communicate Plans**: Let family, friends, or your boss know about the change in schedule. This openness can prevent misunderstandings.
3. **Avoid Panic Mode**: Take a moment to breathe and decide your next steps calmly. Even in a rush, a short pause can keep you from making impulsive or harmful decisions.
4. **Ask for Support**: If you truly cannot handle the new demand alone, reach out to someone you trust for help or advice.

Flexibility does not mean ignoring your plan; it means adjusting it wisely when necessary.

13.14 Protecting Your Recovery in High-Stress Times

Balancing life can become extra challenging during high-stress periods—like the holidays, big work deadlines, or family gatherings. Keep these pointers in mind:

- **Plan Coping Actions**: Have a set of quick stress relief tactics (a short walk, deep breathing, or a safe friend to call) ready.
- **Create Barriers to Old Habits**: If you feel an urge to slip into old harmful patterns, remind yourself of the serious consequences. Keep harmful items out of reach or avoid certain places.
- **Stick to Basic Routines**: Even if your schedule is full, try to keep mealtimes, bedtimes, and short self-care moments consistent. This predictability helps reduce anxiety.

Remember that stress is part of life, but it does not have to derail your progress if you plan and remain aware.

13.15 Less-Known Tips for a Balanced Life

Below are some suggestions that go beyond the usual "make a schedule" advice:

1. **Color Coding**: Assign each life area a color. For example, green for work, blue for family tasks, yellow for personal goals. In your planner or phone calendar, mark tasks accordingly. You will see at a glance if one color dominates your week.
2. **The "Two-Item Bucket" Method**: Each day, pick two tasks that absolutely must be done, and one small self-care activity. Once those are complete, anything else is a bonus. This can lower pressure while ensuring key duties and self-care are covered.
3. **Set an Alarm for Bedtime**: Many people set an alarm to wake up, but not for sleeping. By scheduling bedtime, you remind yourself to wind down and get enough rest.

These little tweaks can make a big impact on how you distribute your energy.

13.16 Dealing with Co-Workers or Bosses Who Overreach

Some workplaces blur the lines between personal time and office time. Here's how to respond if your co-workers or superiors expect you to be always available:

- **Polite but Firm Messages**: "I can address that tomorrow during work hours," or "I have other commitments after 6 p.m., but I'll handle it first thing in the morning."
- **Use Away Messages**: If you have a work email or instant messaging system, set a clear away or offline status when you are off duty.
- **Request a Policy**: If this is a recurring problem for many employees, discuss creating a policy on after-hours contact.

Respecting your boundaries at work is a big step in maintaining life balance. While not all workplaces allow this easily, small efforts can still help.

13.17 Checking in with Yourself Regularly

Balance is not a one-time fix. It is an ongoing practice. Schedule regular self-checks to see if your life is leaning too far in any direction:

1. **Monthly Reflection**: Ask yourself questions like, "Am I feeling too tired or stressed? Have I made time for friends or enjoyable activities?"
2. **Sign of Imbalance**: Excessive irritability, trouble sleeping, forgetting tasks, or feeling a strong urge to retreat from responsibilities might indicate you are overwhelmed.
3. **Adjust Based on Needs**: If you find you are working too much, scale back if possible. If you realize you have not spent enough time with loved ones, plan a get-together or shared activity.

Being proactive about re-balancing can prevent small issues from growing into serious problems.

13.18 Key Points from Chapter 13

1. Striking a balance among work, home responsibilities, and personal free time is crucial to long-term stability.
2. Listing your roles and duties provides a clear map of what needs attention.
3. Setting boundaries and realistic expectations protects you from overcommitment and fatigue.
4. Time-blocking and delegation help ensure that tasks are handled without sacrificing rest or social connection.
5. Work should not dominate your life; clearly define off-hours and take necessary breaks.
6. Creating a calm home environment with routines and shared calendars lowers daily tension.
7. Scheduling free time is essential—rest is not a luxury but a vital part of self-care.
8. Feelings of guilt about taking breaks can be replaced with reminders that rest boosts overall well-being.
9. Social activities need planning as well, so they do not clash with your budget or schedule.
10. Being present with family and friends means switching off distractions and listening actively.
11. Avoid swings between all work and all rest by aiming for consistent daily habits.
12. Unexpected events can happen; adapt calmly, communicate changes, and ask for help if needed.
13. Protect your recovery during high-stress times by having coping methods ready and sticking to key routines.
14. Color coding tasks, using a two-item priority list, and setting a bedtime alarm are unique ways to maintain balance.
15. If bosses or co-workers overreach, polite but firm messages about your off-hours can help keep your boundaries.
16. Regular self-checks and adjustments maintain balance over the long run.

Conclusion
Balancing the different parts of your life is a continuous process. It requires honest self-awareness, practical scheduling, and, often, some negotiation with the people around you. By learning to handle work, home responsibilities, and

rest in a measured way, you give yourself the best chance to stay safe from relapse, reduce daily anxiety, and nurture stronger relationships.

These principles pair well with the problem-solving and communication skills discussed in earlier chapters. As you practice them, you will find that you have more space to breathe and more energy to put toward the things that truly matter. In the next chapter, we will explore ways to find and maintain meaning, even when life throws uncertainties at you. Balancing your day-to-day tasks sets the stage for deeper purpose and fulfillment in the midst of change.

CHAPTER 14: FINDING MEANING IN THE MIDDLE OF UNCERTAINTY

Introduction
Life is often unpredictable. Jobs shift, relationships evolve, and personal goals can change. After leaving a harmful habit behind, you might experience moments when you ask, "What is this all for?" or "Where do I go now?" Finding meaning does not always mean having a grand plan; it can come from smaller but powerful sources—like supporting someone in need, engaging in spiritual or philosophical reflection, or discovering personal growth through every challenge.

This chapter will delve into how to stay purposeful even when things feel shaky. You will learn methods for clarifying your values, using setbacks as opportunities for deeper insight, and locating small yet significant ways to contribute to the world around you. By concentrating on what truly matters to you, you can face life's uncertainties without constantly feeling lost or tempted to fall back on old habits for solace.

14.1 Understanding the Role of Purpose in Recovery

Meaning or purpose can act as a motivator to keep moving forward during hard times. Here is how it helps:

1. **Inspires Consistency**: A strong sense of why you are doing something makes it easier to maintain routines, resist cravings, and endure discomfort.
2. **Builds Resilience**: When you believe in a cause or see a bigger reason for your actions, you are more likely to bounce back from failures or disappointments.
3. **Reduces Emptiness**: Part of the reason some people engage in harmful habits is to fill a void. Meaningful activities or beliefs can fill that void in a healthier way.

Having a sense of purpose is not about ignoring pain or worries. It is about having a guiding light that helps you navigate through them.

14.2 Identifying Your Personal Values

Values are the principles and ideals that matter most to you. They might include honesty, kindness, creativity, family, learning, or supporting your community. When you align daily choices with these values, life can feel more meaningful:

- **Make a Values List**: Write down any word or phrase that resonates: "trust," "helping others," "growing my skills," "being present with loved ones."
- **Pick Your Top Five**: If you have many, narrow them to the ones you feel truly define how you want to live.
- **Check Alignment**: Ask if your current routine and goals match these values. If "helping others" is key, are you finding ways to do that each week?

By clarifying your values, you have a benchmark for making decisions and setting objectives that genuinely feed a sense of purpose.

14.3 Accepting That Uncertainty Is Part of Life

Some people are unsettled by the fact that not everything can be controlled or predicted. Yet, trying to force absolute certainty can lead to disappointment. Instead:

1. **Recognize the Limits of Control**: You can shape your own actions and mindset, but you cannot always dictate outcomes or what others do.
2. **Embrace Flexibility**: If a plan does not work out, it is not necessarily your fault. You can adjust and find a different path.
3. **Stay in the Present**: When uncertainty feels overwhelming, ground yourself in the current moment—notice your surroundings, your breath, and one positive thing in your environment.

A key part of growth is learning that uncertainty does not mean doom. It often opens doors for new perspectives and learning.

14.4 Finding Small Sources of Fulfillment

Meaning does not have to come from grand achievements. Everyday actions can bring a sense of worth:

- **Acts of Kindness**: Doing a favor for a friend, checking in on a neighbor, or sharing comforting words online can remind you that you make a difference, even in small ways.
- **Personal Growth**: Reading a chapter of a helpful book, practicing a skill, or taking a short online class shows you are evolving.
- **Enjoying Nature or Art**: A walk in a park, watching a sunrise, or listening to a calming piece of music can spark a sense of awe or gratitude.
- **Moments of Connection**: Genuine chats with people who understand you can make you feel valued and remind you that you are part of a bigger human circle.

Recognizing these small but meaningful moments builds a daily life that feels more whole and less reliant on external thrills or harmful behaviors.

14.5 Exploring Spiritual or Reflective Practices

For some individuals, meaning is tied to a spiritual path, a faith community, or reflective exercises like meditation. However, you do not have to follow a religion to gain insight from reflective practices:

- **Meditation or Quiet Time**: Spending even five minutes focusing on your breath or a peaceful image can calm the mind and let deeper questions come forward.
- **Journaling**: Write about your hopes, fears, or any insights you discover about yourself. This can shine a light on what matters to you and where you find meaning.
- **Reading Spiritual or Philosophical Texts**: If you are drawn to certain writings, they might offer perspectives that help you see beyond daily stress.
- **Community or Group Discussions**: Some people find purpose in discussing life questions with a supportive group. Check if there are local meetups, online forums, or workshops.

Reflective practices let you connect with yourself and sometimes with a broader sense of existence or community values.

14.6 Turning Setbacks into Meaningful Lessons

Every bump in the road can be a chance to learn something new about who you are and what you need:

1. **Ask What Went Wrong**: Did a lapse happen because of stress at work, misunderstanding in a relationship, or ignoring self-care? Identifying the root cause can give you a blueprint for improvement.
2. **Apply Insights**: Turn that lesson into a practical change. For example, if a conflict arises because of weak communication, commit to practicing better listening or clearer expressions of your feelings.
3. **Recognize Growth**: Even if the situation was unpleasant, spotting how you have changed or improved since last year can boost your faith that you are evolving in a positive direction.

By viewing setbacks as data points rather than final verdicts, you transform difficulties into stepping stones for deeper purpose and personal development.

14.7 Contributing to the Larger Community

Sometimes, the best way to break out of self-focused anxiety is to look outward. Helping others can be a powerful source of meaning:

- **Volunteer Work**: Whether at an animal shelter, a food bank, a youth program, or an event that raises funds for health causes, giving your time can show you that you are part of something bigger.
- **Peer Support**: If you are further along in recovery, offering support or advice to newcomers can remind you of how far you have come and reaffirm the value of your path.
- **Activism or Advocacy**: If you have a cause you care about—like environmental conservation, mental health awareness, or community justice—lending your voice or effort can increase your sense of purpose.

Contributing to the community does not just benefit others; it also reinforces your sense of belonging and value.

14.8 Building a Future-Oriented Perspective

It is difficult to feel purposeful if you are always looking backward at mistakes. Shifting to a future-oriented mindset can help:

1. **Longer-Term Goals**: Identify something you want to achieve in six months or a year, be it academic, career-related, or personal—like learning a new skill.
2. **Milestones**: Break that goal into mini-steps you can check off. Celebrating each step (using safe, healthy rewards) can keep you motivated.
3. **Visual Reminders**: Place photos, quotes, or notes related to your goal where you will see them daily—on a desk, a fridge, or a phone screen.

Shaping a positive future image can keep you from getting stuck in old patterns or from drifting without direction.

14.9 Coping with the Fear of the Unknown

The unknown can feel scary, especially if you used to rely on harmful behaviors to numb or distract you. Strategies to handle that fear:

- **Take Small Risks**: Practice doing small things that feel uncertain, like trying a new hobby or speaking in a small group. Each success builds confidence in facing the unknown.
- **Prepare What You Can**: If you are anxious about a potential problem (like a job interview or an upcoming medical test), gather information and plan. Knowledge can reduce irrational fears.
- **Talk It Through**: Sharing your worries with a supportive friend or therapist can give you fresh perspectives and reduce the power of your anxieties.

Facing uncertainty step by step often makes it less intimidating over time.

14.10 Creating Personal Rituals

Rituals are simple repeated actions that hold special meaning for you. They can mark transitions in your day or honor personal milestones:

- **Morning Reflection**: Each day, write a short sentence about something you look forward to or appreciate.
- **End-of-Week Review**: On a chosen day, review what went well, what was challenging, and what you learned.
- **Anniversary Rituals**: Mark the date you quit your harmful habit or overcame a tough event. Maybe light a candle, take a mindful walk, or write yourself an encouraging note about how far you have come.
- **Seasonal Traditions**: Create your own simple ways to greet each new season—like a day for cleaning and organizing or setting fresh intentions.

These rituals add structure and provide gentle reminders of the path you are on, helping you stay grounded when external conditions seem shaky.

14.11 Balancing Personal Meaning with Practical Needs

Sometimes, focusing on big questions about purpose might clash with the demands of daily life—paying bills, cooking meals, or dealing with a tough job. Balance can be found through:

- **Integrating Meaning into Routine**: For example, if you value creativity, find small ways to express it in your cooking, your workspace decoration, or your short break doodles.
- **Quiet Moments**: Even five minutes of calm reflection can fit around your job or family schedule.
- **Quality Over Quantity**: You do not need hours for deep thought daily. Ten focused minutes of journaling can be more beneficial than an entire day of distraction.

Remember, you are allowed to aim for purpose while still handling the practical realities of living.

14.12 Overcoming Cynicism and Self-Doubt

Many people wrestle with the voice that says, "I can't really change anything," or "None of this matters." Counter it by:

1. **Examining Evidence**: Think about times when your actions did make a difference—to a friend, a family member, a project at work.
2. **Seeking Inspiring Stories**: Learn about people who overcame major hurdles, or read accounts of small acts of kindness that had real impact.
3. **Testing Small Changes**: Prove your cynicism wrong with a direct experiment. Maybe volunteer for a small local cause and see how your presence helps.

Self-doubt often loses power when faced with real-life examples of positive change.

14.13 Allowing Yourself to Evolve

As you move forward, your sense of meaning might shift. A job you once loved may start to feel unfulfilling, or a hobby may no longer bring you joy. It is okay to change course:

- **Periodic Check-Ins**: Every few months, ask yourself, "Are my interests or goals shifting? How can I adjust my path accordingly?"
- **Avoid Inertia**: Staying in an unfulfilling situation just because it feels familiar can reopen old wounds or lead to risky behaviors.
- **Embrace Growth**: Part of living a purposeful life is understanding that change is normal. As you gain new insights, your direction might adjust, and that can be a sign of healthy development.

Evolving does not mean you are inconsistent; it means you are staying true to who you are becoming.

14.14 Connecting with Others on a Similar Search

Sometimes, you might feel alone in your quest to find meaning, especially if your friends or family do not share the same interests or reflections. However:

- **Support Groups**: Many groups exist for people seeking a more meaningful life or trying to maintain healthier habits. You might find one that resonates with you in person or online.
- **Study or Discussion Circles**: Some community centers or libraries host groups that read and discuss books on self-improvement, spirituality, or philosophy.
- **Online Communities**: Even if you cannot attend in person, forums or social media groups can provide a sense of belonging. Just be mindful to pick positive, constructive spaces.

Talking about life's deeper questions with people who understand can reinforce your sense of direction and commitment.

14.15 Less-Known Ideas for Finding Meaning

Here are a few unique suggestions:

1. **Create a Personal Mission Statement**: Summarize in one or two sentences what drives you. For example, "I aim to grow kindness in myself and others through my words and actions." Read it daily.
2. **Acts of Micro-Bravery**: Do small, brave things regularly, like striking up a conversation with someone new, trying a small creative project, or speaking up about an issue that concerns you. Each act boosts confidence and helps you see meaning in taking a stand.
3. **Encourage Others Secretly**: Send an anonymous note of support or do a small good deed without taking credit. Sometimes the quiet knowledge that you have improved someone's day can be deeply fulfilling.

These ideas can spark new ways of seeing how you can add value to your own life and to the lives of others.

14.16 Combining Meaning with Recovery Tools

All the strategies you learned in earlier chapters—handling stress, balancing your schedule, using constructive self-talk—can merge with a sense of purpose:

- **Calendar of Purpose**: Alongside tasks for work or home, note a "purpose action" each week—like a volunteer shift, a reflection session, or a small kindness act.
- **Tie Goals to Values**: If one of your core values is "helping others," you might set a goal to help a friend or neighbor weekly.
- **Use Meaning to Counter Urges**: When a craving arises, remind yourself, "I'm living for something bigger than this immediate urge. My actions today shape the meaningful life I want."

Linking daily tasks with broader meaning strengthens both your commitment to staying on a safer path and your sense of fulfillment.

14.17 Dealing with Periods of Doubt or Emotional Slumps

Even the most motivated person can experience phases where meaning feels distant. If that happens:

1. **Check Physical Needs**: Low energy could be due to lack of sleep, poor diet, or high stress. Address those first.
2. **Simplify**: If you feel overwhelmed, temporarily scale back on big existential questions. Focus on small daily tasks or mini-goals to regain momentum.
3. **Seek Guidance**: A counselor, trusted friend, or group leader might offer fresh insights. Sometimes, an outside perspective helps you see that your struggle is normal and temporary.

Periods of doubt are part of the human experience. They do not erase the value of your journey; they just remind you to adjust and realign.

14.18 Key Points from Chapter 14

1. Purpose can fuel consistency in recovery, build resilience, and fill the void that once fed harmful habits.
2. Clarifying personal values helps shape daily decisions that support deeper meaning.
3. Accepting uncertainty frees you from the stress of trying to control everything and allows for flexible growth.
4. Small, daily acts—kindness, learning, connecting with nature—can foster a sense of value.
5. Spiritual or reflective practices, such as meditation or journaling, offer space to explore deeper questions.
6. Setbacks can become stepping stones if you analyze them for lessons and use those insights to evolve.
7. Contributing to community through volunteering or mentoring strengthens your sense of being part of something bigger.
8. Shifting focus to the future and setting milestones can combat the aimlessness that sometimes follows giving up a harmful habit.
9. Fear of the unknown can be tackled by practicing small risks, gathering information, and seeking supportive voices.
10. Personal rituals bring structure and can anchor you in times of change or doubt.
11. Merge meaning with practicality by weaving purposeful actions into your everyday routines.
12. Combat cynicism through real examples of positive change and by testing small improvements in your own life.
13. Allow your sense of purpose to evolve as you grow and discover new interests or insights.
14. Seek like-minded communities that share your drive to live with deeper significance.
15. Keep using your recovery tools—balanced scheduling, self-talk, problem-solving—while adding purpose as an extra layer of motivation.
16. Recognize that doubt and slumps happen. Address basic needs, simplify goals, and lean on trustworthy companions for support when they occur.

Conclusion
Finding meaning in the middle of uncertainty is not always straightforward, but it is well worth the effort. By focusing on your values, staying open to learning,

and looking for small ways to feel purposeful each day, you can craft a life that feels richer and more resilient against the ebb and flow of challenges. Your sense of meaning does not have to be grand or final—allow it to grow and shift along with your experiences.

This chapter closes another layer of understanding on your path to a steadier life after addiction. In the chapters ahead, we will explore how to handle anger and frustration (Chapter 15) and the importance of supportive systems and role models (Chapter 16). Each part of this book is designed to help you build a well-rounded skill set for ongoing growth, even when life remains unpredictable. By blending a sense of purpose with the practical methods you have been learning, you can face the future with a stronger sense of stability and a healthier view of your place in the world.

CHAPTER 15: HANDLING ANGER AND FRUSTRATION

Introduction
Anger and frustration are normal human emotions, but they can grow intense in life after harmful habits. At times, you might feel as though you have reached a boiling point. Maybe someone's words spark a memory of past hurts, or you find yourself irritated by small things that once barely registered. How you deal with anger can either support your healthier path or threaten to pull you back into destructive responses.

In this chapter, we will look at practical methods for recognizing anger early, controlling it before it controls you, and channeling its energy into safer actions. We will also discuss how to handle long-standing resentment, manage conflicts without exploding, and forgive yourself when you slip into anger in a way you regret. Anger is not simply a "bad" emotion. It can alert you that something is wrong or that your needs are not being met. The goal is not to block anger entirely, but to handle it so it does not damage your progress, relationships, or sense of self-worth.

15.1 Understanding Anger's Purpose

Anger can serve as a signal that something feels unfair, unsafe, or in violation of your values:

- **Alert**: It tells you that someone or something might be harming you, crossing a boundary, or disrespecting you.
- **Energy Source**: It can give a burst of energy to face a threat, solve a problem, or stand up for yourself.
- **Indicator of Inner Wounds**: Sometimes, anger shows that an old hurt is still raw. Recognizing this can point you toward deeper emotional healing.

However, if anger remains unregulated—turning into yelling, violence, or self-harm—it can unravel the positive steps you have taken. Anger, when handled carefully, can lead to constructive action. When it is allowed to explode, it can create more chaos and regret.

15.2 Common Triggers for Anger and Frustration

Anger triggers can be unique to each person. Here are a few common ones:

1. **Feeling Disrespected**: Someone talking down to you or ignoring your needs can stir up strong resentment.
2. **Unmet Expectations**: When you expect something to happen (like a friend showing up on time) and it does not, frustration might flare.
3. **Stress Overload**: Lack of sleep, financial worries, or tense relationships can leave you on edge, making you prone to snap over small issues.
4. **Memories of Past Hurt**: A tone of voice, a smell, or a situation similar to old traumatic events can bring anger forward.

Identifying your triggers is a key step in managing your reactions. The next time you feel angry out of the blue, consider if it may be linked to one of these or other triggers.

15.3 Early Warning Signs of Anger

Anger often builds gradually. Recognizing early physical and mental signs can help you stop it from escalating:

- **Physical Clues**: Your heart rate speeds up, your jaw or fists clench, and you might feel heat in your face or neck.
- **Mental Shifts**: Racing thoughts like, "They can't do this to me," or "I'm fed up," might dominate your mind.
- **Emotional Tension**: A wave of irritability or the desire to lash out verbally.

When you notice these clues, you can take steps to cool down instead of letting the anger spiral.

15.4 Basic Methods for Cooling Down

If you catch anger in its early stage, try these simple methods:

1. **Take a Pause**: Stop what you are doing and count to 10 (or 20 if you need more time). This gives you a moment to gather yourself.
2. **Deep Breathing**: Inhale for a slow count of four, hold briefly, exhale for a slow count of four. Repeat a few times. This calms your nervous system and lowers physical tension.
3. **Body Movement**: A brisk walk around the block, a short set of jumping jacks, or even squeezing a stress ball can release some of the pent-up energy.
4. **Drink Water**: Sipping water can provide a short break, both mentally and physically.

These small actions may sound too basic, but they can prevent the anger wave from growing into a bigger storm.

15.5 Techniques to Manage Anger Long-Term

If you struggle often with anger, consider more structured approaches:

- **Anger Journaling**: Write down events that made you angry, how you reacted, and how you felt afterward. Notice patterns—like certain words or topics that set you off.
- **Regular Physical Activity**: Activities like walking, running, or yoga can regulate mood and provide a safe outlet for tension.
- **Relaxation Routines**: Practicing short relaxation exercises daily (not just when angry) can lower your baseline stress, making you less reactive.
- **Talking to a Professional**: A counselor or therapist can help you explore underlying causes of anger, like past traumas or unhealthy thought patterns.

Remember, anger is not a sign of weakness; it is a human emotion. Learning to channel it effectively is part of emotional growth.

15.6 Assertive Communication Instead of Lashing Out

Sometimes anger comes from feeling unheard or misunderstood. Learning to express your views assertively can reduce the build-up of frustration:

1. **Calm Statement of Concern**: Instead of yelling, "You never listen to me!" try, "I feel unheard when I speak and there's no reply. I need to feel you understand me."
2. **Focus on the Issue**: Keep the discussion centered on the current problem. Avoid dragging in old hurts or blaming the other person's character.
3. **Propose Solutions**: Suggest ways to fix the situation. It might be as simple as, "Could we set aside 10 minutes each day to talk about how we're doing?"

Assertiveness shows respect for both yourself and the other person, which can stop anger from exploding into insults or harsh words.

15.7 Handling Resentment and Grudges

Resentment is anger that lingers over time, often directed at someone who hurt you or let you down. It can silently corrode your peace. To deal with it:

- **Acknowledge It**: Admit that you still harbor anger instead of pretending everything is fine.
- **Identify What You Need**: Do you need an apology, a conversation to clear the air, or a change in the situation? Sometimes, the person might never give you what you want, so you may need to find closure on your own.
- **Let Go of the Fantasy of Revenge**: Holding onto thoughts of payback keeps you stuck. It often does more harm to you than to the other person.
- **Seek Support**: Talking with a counselor or a trusted group can help you process old anger and move forward without carrying resentment's weight.

Letting go of resentment does not excuse the wrong that happened; it just means you choose to free yourself from its grip.

15.8 Anger in Family or Close Relationships

Family members can trigger your temper in ways others cannot because they often know which buttons to press. Some strategies:

1. **Agree on Limits**: If someone starts yelling or insulting you, let them know calmly that you will leave the conversation if the disrespect continues.
2. **Pick the Right Time**: Serious topics should not be discussed when everyone is tired or in a rush. Plan a talk when both sides can focus.
3. **Take Pauses During Heated Talks**: If the argument escalates, pause. Say, "I need to step away for a moment to calm down, but I do want to finish this conversation."
4. **Practice Empathy**: Family members have their own stress or past wounds. While this does not excuse bad behavior, understanding it might ease some anger and lead to solutions.

Family anger can be deeply rooted, so patience and repeated efforts to stay calm might be necessary.

15.9 Anger and Relapse Risks

Anger is a common relapse trigger because it can push you to seek relief. Recognizing this:

- **HALT Check**: Ask if you are Hungry, Angry, Lonely, or Tired. These states can raise the chance of old, harmful coping.
- **Recovery Plan**: If you feel your anger rising, quickly use the tools you have (call a friend, do a calming exercise, attend a support meeting).
- **Self-Talk**: Remind yourself that giving in to old habits will not fix the problem causing your anger. It might even worsen it.
- **Positive Release**: Keep a list of safe outlets—writing a journal entry, punching a cushion, going for a run, or talking to a mentor.

Anger does not have to derail your progress. See it as a warning sign that you need to act in a healthier way.

15.10 Healthy Outlets for Anger

Instead of letting anger burn inside, find safer expressions:

1. **Creative Activities**: Drawing, painting, or writing music can let you release strong feelings.
2. **Physical Exercise**: High-energy exercise can burn off the adrenaline that comes with anger.
3. **Talking with a Friend**: Expressing your concerns out loud can stop them from growing larger in your mind.
4. **Constructive Action**: If the anger is about an injustice or problem in your community, channel it into volunteering, advocacy, or writing letters to relevant authorities.

A safe outlet can transform anger into fuel for positive change rather than letting it harm you or others.

15.11 Advanced Anger Management Techniques

For deeper work on anger, here are some structured ideas:

- **Cognitive Reframing**: When a situation irritates you, pause and see if your thoughts are exaggerated. For example, thinking "They always ignore me!" can be changed to "They did not respond this time, but sometimes they do."
- **Problem-Solving Steps**: If anger arises from an ongoing issue (like messy housemates), map out solutions. Have a calm discussion, make a chores list, or ask a neutral friend to mediate.
- **Body Scan**: When anger stirs, close your eyes for a moment and mentally check your body from head to toe. Notice tight muscles. Release tension as you go. This can lower the intensity of the feeling.
- **Regular Stress Maintenance**: Keep daily stress in check. The more stress you carry, the easier it is for anger to flare. Practice relaxation or time management to reduce overall tension.

These techniques require consistency, but over time they can retrain your mind and body to respond calmly.

15.12 Dealing with Your Own Mistakes in Anger

No one is perfect. You may lose your temper and say or do things you regret. The key is to:

1. **Accept Responsibility**: Acknowledge what you did or said without blaming others. "I handled that poorly, and I'm sorry."
2. **Apologize Sincerely**: A real apology focuses on making things right, not on justifying your anger.
3. **Repair the Damage**: If your outburst caused harm—like breaking someone's item or hurting them emotionally—ask how you can fix it or make amends.
4. **Learn for Next Time**: Reflect on the trigger, your reaction, and how you can respond differently in the future. This might mean using earlier cool-down steps or stepping away sooner.

Mistakes can be lessons if you address them openly and adjust your behavior.

15.13 Handling Frustration with Yourself

You might get mad at yourself for not meeting personal standards, making slow progress, or repeating unhelpful patterns:

- **Show Self-Compassion**: Talk to yourself as you would talk to a friend. Replace harsh criticisms with balanced statements, like, "I made an error, but I am working on improving."
- **Set Realistic Goals**: If your goals are too big or too many, you set yourself up for disappointment. Break them into smaller steps.
- **Track Progress**: Keep a simple log of your achievements, no matter how small. This reminds you that you are making headway, even if you are not perfect.
- **Seek Encouragement**: When you are frustrated, talk to a trusted mentor or friend who can remind you of your strengths.

Your growth is a process, and frustration at yourself is a sign that you care about doing better. Just do not let it turn into constant self-attack.

15.14 Dealing with Public Anger

Feeling anger in public—like a heated moment at a store, on public transport, or during a meeting—can be embarrassing or even risky:

1. **Quick Exit if Possible**: If you can, step away for a moment. Go to a restroom or outside to breathe and compose yourself.
2. **Inner Self-Talk**: Silently repeat a calming phrase, like, "Stay calm, it's not worth it."
3. **Keep Voice Low**: If you must speak, keep your voice level. This can signal to bystanders and the other party that you are not looking for a fight.
4. **Decide if It's Worth Arguing**: Public conflicts can escalate quickly. If the issue is not urgent, walk away. Handle the problem later in a calmer setting.

Protecting your recovery and safety is more important than proving a point to a stranger or minor situation.

15.15 Role of Forgiveness in Anger Management

Some people misunderstand forgiveness, thinking it means saying the harm was okay. In reality, forgiveness is letting go of the need to stay angry:

- **Forgiveness as Release**: By choosing to forgive, you free yourself from carrying anger about something you cannot change.
- **Internal Process**: The other person does not even have to be involved. Forgiveness can happen entirely within you.
- **Helps You, Not Just Them**: Holding a grudge weighs you down; letting it go can bring relief and free up emotional energy.

It might take time. Forgiveness does not happen instantly, but it can be a major relief once you reach that point.

15.16 When Anger Hides Sadness or Fear

Sometimes, anger is a mask for deeper emotions like sadness, shame, or fear. You might find it easier to feel anger than to face pain or vulnerability. If you sense this:

- **Ask Yourself**: "Am I really angry, or am I hurt/scared underneath?"
- **Safe Expression**: Try talking to a counselor, journaling, or discussing with a friend. Exploring your sadness or fear can reduce the raw anger you feel on the surface.
- **Seek Professional Help if Trauma Is Involved**: Past trauma can result in anger flashes. A mental health professional can guide you through specialized support.

Recognizing hidden emotions can open the door to deeper healing.

15.17 Helping Someone Else Who Is Angry

If you are around someone who is often angry, you might want to help them without getting caught in their storm:

- **Listen Calmly**: Sometimes they just need someone to hear their concerns. Resist the urge to fix or argue immediately.
- **Encourage Resources**: Suggest they talk to a counselor, join an anger management group, or learn breathing techniques.
- **Set Boundaries**: Protect yourself from verbal or physical harm. If they refuse to respect your limits, you may need distance for your own well-being.
- **Avoid Matching Their Anger**: Responding to anger with anger often escalates the conflict. If you remain calm, it might reduce tension.

You can offer support, but remember you are not responsible for fixing another person's anger if they refuse to work on it.

15.18 Key Points from Chapter 15

1. Anger is normal but becomes a problem when it grows too strong or leads to harmful actions.
2. Identifying triggers and early signs helps you respond before anger gets out of control.
3. Basic cool-down methods—such as counting to 10, breathing exercises, or taking a brief walk—can break the initial rush.

4. Long-term tools include journaling, therapy, and a daily routine to keep stress lower.
5. Assertive communication can prevent anger from building up into outbursts.
6. Resentment is prolonged anger that can harm your peace; look for ways to release it rather than letting it fester.
7. Family anger often has deep roots; consistent calm boundaries and empathy can help.
8. Anger can be a relapse trigger; have a plan to handle it safely if it arises.
9. Healthy outlets—like creative expression or physical activity—offer a release for built-up tension.
10. Mistakes in anger should be acknowledged with sincere apologies and concrete steps to improve.
11. Public anger requires quick coping skills to avoid worse trouble.
12. Forgiveness is about freeing yourself from anger's grip, not saying a wrong was okay.
13. Sometimes anger covers deeper hurt or fear; exploring those feelings might reduce the anger.
14. Helping an angry friend or loved one involves calm listening, suggesting resources, and protecting your own boundaries.

Conclusion
Dealing with anger and frustration is about awareness, practical tools, and ongoing practice. Anger is not inherently harmful—it is how you channel it that matters. By learning to sense it early, calm it down, and express it in healthy ways, you protect your relationships, your well-being, and your progress in recovery. As you practice these strategies, anger becomes less of a threat to your mental or emotional health and more of a signal that helps you understand and protect yourself without hurting others.

The next chapter, Chapter 16, looks at building strong support networks and finding positive role models. Having caring people around you and seeing others model healthy behaviors can help you remain stable when anger or other challenges arise. Combining anger management skills with a supportive circle boosts your odds of staying on a safer, more confident path.

CHAPTER 16: SUPPORT SYSTEMS AND POSITIVE ROLE MODELS

Introduction
Life after addiction often feels like standing on new ground. You have broken away from a damaging habit, but you might still feel shaky. In these times, a strong support network can become a lifeline, offering understanding, accountability, and encouragement. Positive role models also show you, through their actions, that lasting growth is possible.

This chapter discusses how to build a network of helpful people—be it friends, family, group leaders, counselors, or online communities—and how to learn from role models who have walked a similar road. You will learn which qualities to look for in a supportive person, how to foster those relationships, and how to avoid connections that could pull you back into old ways. By surrounding yourself with individuals who respect your journey and model healthy living, you increase your chances of staying grounded, even when challenges press in.

16.1 Why Support Systems Matter in Recovery

There is a saying that "no one does it alone." This might be extra true for someone leaving harmful habits behind. A support system can:

1. **Provide Emotional Safety**: When you feel stressed, confused, or sad, a supportive person or group can listen without harsh judgment.
2. **Offer Practical Help**: They might give you a ride to meetings, help you find job leads, or offer tips on handling everyday hurdles.
3. **Celebrate Milestones**: They can notice and honor your progress, which boosts motivation when you feel low.
4. **Help Identify Warnings**: They may spot changes in your behavior that indicate risk, like increased moodiness or isolation, and bring it to your attention.

No matter how strong-willed you are, having allies increases your resilience and helps you see options you might miss on your own.

16.2 Different Types of Support

Support can come in various forms, each offering something unique:

- **Close Friends and Family**: People who know your history and can provide consistent emotional backing.
- **Recovery Groups**: Group meetings or online forums where you connect with others who are on a similar path. Hearing real stories of change can give you hope and practical pointers.
- **Professional Help**: Counselors, therapists, social workers, or doctors who use their expertise to guide you through mental health, financial, or medical challenges.
- **Spiritual or Community Leaders**: If you have a faith or a community center, leaders there might offer mentorship, moral support, or resources.
- **Peer Mentors**: Individuals who have successfully overcome addiction or similar difficulties and can share their personal experiences and coping methods.

Each type can fill a different need. You do not have to limit yourself to just one. In fact, combining support from multiple areas can strengthen your safety net.

16.3 How to Identify Supportive People

Not everyone who appears kind is good for you in the long run. To figure out if someone is truly supportive:

1. **Do They Listen More Than They Judge?** A supportive friend or mentor tries to understand your feelings rather than simply labeling them as good or bad.
2. **Are They Trustworthy?** Look at whether they keep private matters confidential and act in ways that match their words.
3. **Respect for Your Boundaries**: A good supporter will honor your comfort zone and not push you into risky situations.
4. **Positive Influence**: Do they encourage healthy behaviors or drag you back into old patterns? Do they help you see your strengths or do they belittle you?

Spotting these traits helps you choose relationships that nurture your new, safer life rather than sabotage it.

16.4 Finding and Joining Support Groups

Support groups—whether local or virtual—are often a cornerstone for people leaving harmful habits behind. Here is how you can find one:

- **Online Searches**: Look up groups focused on your type of addiction or mental health concern.
- **Local Community Centers**: They may host 12-step programs or other recovery meetings.
- **Counselor Referrals**: Therapists often know well-run groups in your area.
- **Hospital or Clinic Boards**: Some medical facilities have bulletin boards or websites listing support resources.

When you attend, observe the atmosphere. Do members treat each other with care? Are discussions balanced? If you feel safe and welcomed, that group could become part of your support structure.

16.5 Building a Core Circle of Positive Contacts

Not everyone needs to be in your inner circle. It might be best to keep it small and stable:

1. **Select Trusted Individuals**: Choose people you can call or text if you are feeling tempted or upset. Let them know they are part of your core circle.
2. **Establish Contact Frequency**: Some friends may be fine talking once a week, while others are open to daily check-ins. Be clear about what you need.
3. **Mix Personal and Group Support**: You might have one close family member, a friend from a recovery group, and perhaps a sponsor or mentor. Having variety can help you see problems from different angles.
4. **Agree on Boundaries**: Ask your core supporters how they prefer to help (listening, problem-solving, giving a ride, etc.). Also clarify what is off-limits, like late-night calls if they have an early job.

A stable circle can act like a shield against isolation and destructive urges.

16.6 Learning from Positive Role Models

A role model is someone whose life or behavior you admire and want to learn from. This does not mean they are perfect, but they have qualities or experiences that can guide you:

- **Traits to Observe**: How do they handle stress, speak to others, manage setbacks, and make decisions? What daily habits keep them on track?
- **Ask for Insight**: If it is someone you know, you can ask, "How did you handle this kind of challenge?" or "What helped you stay focused?"
- **Watch Their Boundaries**: Good role models often show healthy limits with others and themselves. You can learn from their approach to balance.
- **Combine Lessons with Your Style**: You do not have to copy them exactly. Adapt what works for your personal situation.

Seeing that others have walked a similar road successfully can remind you that change is possible and worth the effort.

16.7 The Value of Mentors and Sponsors

In many recovery settings, mentors (or sponsors) are people who have maintained their healthier life for a certain period. They can:

- **Share Real Experience**: They know what it is like to fight cravings, rebuild trust with loved ones, or face unexpected triggers.
- **Check Your Blind Spots**: They might see patterns in your behavior or thinking that you cannot see because you are too close to it.
- **Offer Encouragement**: A mentor can help you keep perspective: "I remember going through that. It does get easier."
- **Provide Accountability**: Knowing you have someone to report to can give you an extra reason to stay on track.

If you seek a mentor, look for someone who is reliable, respectful, and stable in their own recovery.

16.8 Healthy Communication Within Your Support Network

Once you have supporters, it is essential to communicate well:

- **Regular Updates**: Do not wait until a crisis hits. Check in, even briefly, to keep them aware of how you are doing.
- **Honesty**: If you hide struggles out of shame, no one can help you. Be open about tough urges or negative thoughts.
- **Respect Their Time**: Contact them in agreed-upon ways. If they cannot talk right away, find a backup plan, like writing in a journal or reaching out to another friend.
- **Listening to Them Too**: A support system is two-way if possible. Even a mentor may want a friendly ear sometimes. This mutual respect can strengthen the bond.

Clear communication prevents misunderstandings and keeps your connections positive and supportive.

16.9 Avoiding Negative Influences

Not everyone in your orbit will be good for your recovery. You might need to set boundaries or distance yourself from:

- **Peers Who Still Use**: If they keep pushing old substances or behaviors, continuing to hang out with them can be very risky.
- **Chronic Complainers**: People who constantly bring negativity or drama can wear you down, especially when you are in a fragile state.
- **Unsupportive Family Members**: Some relatives might mock your progress or remind you of past failures. If they cannot respect your new direction, consider limiting contact.
- **Toxic Relationships**: Verbal, emotional, or physical mistreatment can trigger dangerous stress. Your safety and growth must come first.

It is not always easy to step away from old friends or family ties, but safeguarding your recovery often requires choosing healthier environments.

16.10 Handling Disagreements or Letdowns in Your Network

Even helpful relationships can experience conflict. You might feel let down if a friend fails to show up or if a mentor disagrees with your choices. When issues arise:

1. **Communicate Calmly**: Use "I" statements. "I felt alone when you did not come," instead of "You never show up."
2. **Seek to Understand Their Side**: Maybe they had an emergency or they think your approach is risky. Ask questions before making assumptions.
3. **Reassess Boundaries**: If the conflict shows a mismatch in expectations, clarify roles or contact frequency.
4. **Consider Counseled Mediation**: If the disagreement is deep, a mediator—like a counselor—can help each side speak safely.

One or two conflicts do not necessarily ruin a good relationship. Open talk and respect can prevent small letdowns from becoming bigger issues.

16.11 Online Support Communities

If in-person groups are not accessible or you prefer more privacy, online communities can also be strong sources of backing:

- **Forums and Chat Groups**: Many recovery-focused forums exist. You can post questions, share your experiences, and get support 24/7.
- **Video Meetings**: Virtual meetups can offer face-to-face contact without leaving home.
- **Social Media Groups**: Private groups on platforms allow members to share milestones or daily challenges.

When joining online groups, be cautious. Some spaces might be unmonitored or prone to conflicts. Look for well-moderated groups that encourage respect and positive interaction.

16.12 Balancing Support with Self-Reliance

Having a network does not mean you depend on others for every decision. It is about finding a balance:

- **Take Personal Responsibility**: Your supporters can guide you, but you must make your own choices.
- **Learn to Self-Soothe**: Practice calming techniques so you do not have to call someone every time a small urge hits.
- **Set Growth Goals**: Work on skills and independence. Over time, you might rely on supporters less for everyday matters but still keep them for deeper crises or accountability.

Healthy independence combined with wise use of support can create a strong platform for long-term well-being.

16.13 Offering Support to Others in Need

A support system thrives when members help one another. You do not have to be fully healed to give someone a listening ear:

- **Share Your Progress**: Telling someone what worked for you can spark hope.
- **Respect Boundaries**: Offer support, but do not push your advice if they do not want it.
- **Watch for Red Flags**: If a friend is in danger, you may need to encourage them to seek professional help or call emergency services.
- **Avoid "Rescuing"**: You cannot fix another person's problems. You can only assist, suggest resources, and show empathy.

Helping others can also reinforce your own commitment to safer habits, as it reminds you how far you have come.

16.14 Recognizing When You Need Expert Intervention

Some issues may exceed what friends or group members can handle. You might need professional help if:

- **You Show Signs of Deep Depression**: Constant hopelessness, loss of interest in daily tasks, or suicidal thoughts.
- **You Experience Crippling Anxiety**: Unable to sleep, eat, or function normally due to fear or panic.

- **Severe Relapse**: If a slip goes on for days or weeks, or you cannot stop yourself from returning to old habits.
- **Legal or Financial Crises**: Owing large sums, facing eviction, or dealing with possible jail time.

In such cases, a trained expert—like a therapist, financial counselor, or legal advisor—can provide targeted solutions and therapy beyond the scope of a typical support circle.

16.15 Less-Known Ways to Strengthen Your Network

You can enhance your support system in creative ways:

1. **Small Group Activities**: Create a hobby group (like a book club or hiking group) where you invite both supportive friends and new acquaintances. This introduces fresh perspectives and connections.
2. **Recovery Retreats**: Some organizations host weekend or day-long events that blend workshops with social bonding. These can deepen friendships in a structured setting.
3. **Skill Exchange**: Trade a skill you have (like guitar lessons or cooking) for a skill someone else has (like job interview prep). It fosters mutual respect and collaboration.

Such activities can enrich your network with people who share your interests or your growth mindset.

16.16 Self-Awareness in Choosing Role Models

Picking the right role models is an active process:

- **Know What You Want to Learn**: Are you seeking better emotional control, career advice, or faith-based guidance? Identify your needs first.
- **Check Alignment**: If someone's style or values clash heavily with yours, they may not be the best example.
- **Observe Action Over Words**: A role model who preaches about honesty but often lies or gossips is not a reliable guide.

- **Stay Open to Multiple Influences**: You might admire one person's work ethic, another person's calmness, and another's communication skills.

By staying aware of your needs and aims, you can gather insights from several role models to form a personalized approach.

16.17 Reviewing and Updating Your Support System

Your network and role models might shift as you grow. It is healthy to update your circle:

1. **Regular Check-Ins**: Every few months, ask, "Are these relationships still supportive? Are there new areas where I need help?"
2. **Thank and Release**: If a certain person is no longer helpful or your bond has faded, you can still appreciate what they provided in the past. You can move on gracefully.
3. **Stay Open to New Arrivals**: A new coworker, neighbor, or group member might become a great supporter if you are willing to welcome them into your circle.
4. **Avoid Overcrowding**: Having too many people in your close circle can make communication hard. Quality often beats quantity.

A flexible approach ensures your support system evolves along with your changing life and goals.

16.18 Key Points from Chapter 16

1. Support networks reduce isolation, offer emotional and practical help, and highlight potential trouble signs in your recovery.
2. Various forms of support—close friends, recovery groups, professionals, and online communities—can all reinforce your progress.
3. Look for people who listen without judging, respect your boundaries, and encourage healthy actions.
4. A core circle of trusted contacts can serve as your emergency line and day-to-day safety net.
5. Positive role models, whether mentors or everyday people, show you how to handle stress and remain stable in healthy ways.

6. Communication within your support system should be honest, consistent, and respectful of each person's time and energy.
7. Negative or toxic influences can sabotage your recovery; limit contact if they refuse to respect your new life.
8. Even good support relationships can face conflicts; handle them with calm dialogue, understanding, and boundary-setting.
9. Online communities provide 24/7 help if in-person meetings are not feasible, but choose reliable, respectful groups.
10. Balancing your reliance on others with building your own independence is key to a strong recovery foundation.
11. You can also strengthen your commitment by helping others in recovery, as long as you keep healthy limits.
12. Recognize signs that you need professional intervention, such as intense depression or repeated, uncontrollable lapses.
13. Enrich your network with new connections through group activities, retreats, or skill exchanges.
14. Choose role models wisely, focusing on actions over mere words. You can learn different skills from multiple sources.
15. Review and adjust your support system as you grow; some relationships fade while new ones arise.
16. A stable network of caring, respectful individuals—backed by role models who inspire you—can keep you grounded even when life challenges reappear.

Conclusion
Building and maintaining a reliable support network, along with identifying good role models, can help secure your progress in life after harmful habits. The people around you can offer guidance, motivation, and a reminder that no one has to face challenges alone. When combined with the coping strategies you have learned—like managing anger (Chapter 15) or finding daily purpose (Chapter 14)—you arm yourself with a robust safety net.

In the upcoming chapters, we will look at how to deal with setbacks and disappointments (Chapter 17) and how to care for your long-term health in mind and body (Chapter 18). Each step of the way, remember that your network can be a source of comfort and direction. Keep an eye out for supportive, understanding people, and stay open to the insights they share. Through strong connections and positive influences, you will find it easier to stand firm on your new ground, ready to face whatever comes next.

CHAPTER 17: DEALING WITH DISAPPOINTMENT AND SETBACKS

Introduction

No matter how well you plan or how hard you work on your mental health after breaking a harmful habit, setbacks can still happen. You might slip up on an important goal, face an unexpected life challenge, or feel the sting of someone's disappointment in you. At times, these moments can feel like heavy blows, especially if you have been trying to stay on a healthier path. However, disappointment and setbacks are not proof that you have failed; they are road bumps that can teach you new skills and strengthen your resolve.

In this chapter, we will look at why setbacks happen, how to deal with the shame and guilt that often follow them, and specific techniques to recover faster. We will also explore practical ways to turn disappointment into a stepping stone rather than a defeat. Setbacks can be scary, but they do not have to derail your progress forever. Learning to handle them with calm, honesty, and strategic thinking can help you protect your mental well-being and stay on track.

17.1 Understanding Why Setbacks Happen

Many people think of setbacks as a personal failure or a sign that they lack willpower. In reality, setbacks often have multiple causes:

1. **Stress Overload**: Excessive stress at work, school, or home might leave you tired and vulnerable.
2. **Lack of Support**: If you find yourself tackling challenges alone, you may fall back into old habits when the pressure mounts.
3. **Sudden Life Events**: A job loss, health scare, or relationship problem can shake your stability.
4. **Overconfidence**: Sometimes, feeling "cured" can lead to risky choices, like hanging out in old harmful environments, which raise the odds of a slip.
5. **Gradual Slips in Self-Care**: Skipping daily calming exercises or ignoring small stress signs might let tension build until you snap.

Recognizing that setbacks are usually the result of multiple factors can reduce self-blame. It also points to areas you can fix or strengthen.

17.2 Immediate Responses to a Setback

When a setback occurs—like a brief return to an old habit or making a mistake at work—you may feel panicked or ashamed. Here are first steps to take:

- **Pause and Breathe**: Stop the mental storm for a moment. Inhale slowly, hold, then exhale. Repeat a few times to clear your head.
- **Acknowledge the Event**: Say (aloud or in your mind), "I slipped," or "I messed up." This honest admission helps you avoid denial.
- **Seek Safe Support**: If possible, reach out to a trusted friend, family member, mentor, or sponsor. A quick talk can stop the slip from growing.
- **Avoid Making It Bigger**: Try not to think, "Now I've ruined everything." A single setback does not erase all your progress.
- **Hold Off on Major Decisions**: Emotions are raw after a disappointment. Avoid drastic choices (like quitting a job or cutting off a relationship) until you feel calmer.

This immediate response focuses on damage control, preventing the setback from spiraling into more harmful behaviors or deeper emotional crisis.

17.3 Common Emotional Reactions to Disappointment

When you feel disappointed by someone else's actions or by your own slip, you might go through a range of emotions:

1. **Guilt and Shame**: You might think, "I should have done better," or "I'm letting everyone down."
2. **Anger or Blame**: Sometimes frustration is turned outward: "This is their fault for not helping me."
3. **Hopelessness**: You might feel stuck, thinking, "Nothing ever works out for me."
4. **Fear of Judgment**: Worrying about how others will react if they learn about your setback.

These emotions can feel overwhelming, but they are normal. Talking them through with a counselor, friend, or in a journal can prevent you from getting stuck in them.

17.4 Separating the Event from Your Self-Worth

A major source of pain after a setback is tying the slip to your identity. You might label yourself as "useless" or "hopeless." Instead:

- **Focus on the Action**: Say, "I made an unhelpful choice," instead of "I am a failure."
- **Recall Past Strengths**: Remind yourself of other times you handled difficult tasks well, or overcame obstacles.
- **Use Balanced Self-Talk**: "Yes, I stumbled here, but I have also done many things right. I can learn and move on."
- **Seek Honest Feedback**: If you are confused about how bad things really are, talk to someone you trust who can give an objective view. Sometimes, we magnify mistakes in our own minds.

By keeping your sense of self separate from the slip, you can maintain confidence in your ability to improve.

17.5 Strategies to Recover from a Slip in Old Habits

One of the toughest setbacks is returning to an addictive habit, even if briefly. Here is a plan to move forward if that occurs:

1. **Stop as Soon as You Can**: If you slipped once, do not let it continue. Halt the behavior right away and remove any triggers, like leftover substance or harmful contacts.
2. **Contact Your Support System**: Inform your trusted allies or sponsor. They can remind you that one lapse does not mean you must fully return to the old habit.
3. **Update Your Prevention Plan**: Look at what allowed the slip. Did you ignore certain triggers? Did you drop your daily self-care steps? Use these insights to refine your plan.

4. **Consider Professional Help**: If the slip led to a more extended lapse or you feel shaky about stopping again, meeting with a counselor or doctor can help you stabilize.
   5. **Practice Self-Forgiveness**: Recognize that stumbles can happen, but they do not define your future.

Treat a slip as urgent but fixable. The faster you address it, the less damage it does.

17.6 Turning Disappointment into Insight

Disappointment—whether it is about failing a personal goal or feeling let down by someone—can become a teacher if you let it:

- **Ask "What Can I Learn?"**: Did I set unrealistic expectations? Did I rely on one person too much?
- **Check Communication**: Did the disappointment arise because I never expressed my needs clearly?
- **List Solutions**: For future situations, how can I set clearer boundaries, balance my workload, or manage my emotions better?
- **Refine Action Steps**: Decide on one or two changes that could prevent the same disappointment from happening again.

Adopting a curious mindset can ease some of the pain by shifting focus to improvement rather than dwelling on regrets.

17.7 Handling Self-Blame vs. External Blame

In moments of setback, blame can get confusing. You might blame yourself for not trying harder or blame others for not supporting you. A balanced approach is helpful:

- **Own Your Choices**: Acknowledge the parts of the setback you could have controlled, like ignoring a warning sign or refusing to ask for help.

- **Recognize External Factors**: Sometimes, outside events do play a role (e.g., losing a job because of company-wide layoffs, not your performance).
- **Aim for Growth**: Instead of drowning in guilt or anger, direct your energy to what you can do next. If you hold onto blame, you might miss practical steps to fix or prevent the issue.

Balance ensures you are neither unfairly punishing yourself nor avoiding honest accountability.

17.8 Coping with Others' Disappointment in You

It is painful when someone you care about feels disappointed because you missed a promise or had a lapse. Here is how to handle it:

1. **Listen Without Defensiveness**: Let them express their feelings. Resist the urge to argue or make excuses right away.
2. **Apologize if Needed**: If you broke a promise or made a mistake that affected them, offer a sincere apology.
3. **Explain Your Plan to Improve**: Show them you are not taking this lightly. Mention the steps you will take to prevent a repeat.
4. **Respect Their Reaction**: They might need time to rebuild trust or accept your apology. Try not to force them to "get over it" instantly.
5. **Keep Communicating**: Over time, consistent actions and open talks can restore faith in your commitment.

Though it can be uncomfortable, facing others' disappointment calmly can heal the relationship and build mutual understanding.

17.9 Building Emotional Resilience

Resilience is the ability to bounce back from setbacks. You can develop it through:

- **Daily Self-Care**: Activities like short walks, deep breathing, light stretching, or simple hobbies reduce overall stress.

- **Challenge Negative Thoughts**: When you catch yourself thinking, "I can't handle this," replace it with, "I can try a different approach or ask for help."
- **Nurture Supportive Ties**: Keep in contact with friends or mentors who believe in your potential.
- **Set Incremental Goals**: Tackle tasks in small steps, recognizing each small win. This grows your sense of capability.
- **Learn from Observing Others**: Notice how people you respect handle failure or heartbreak. Use their methods as inspiration.

Emotional resilience is a skill—like a muscle—that can be strengthened with practice.

17.10 Reassessing Your Goals and Strategies

A setback might show that some of your plans or goals need adjustment:

1. **Simplify or Adjust Targets**: If you aimed too high too soon, break it into smaller steps.
2. **Check Your Daily Routines**: Are you skipping the basics, like enough sleep, healthy meals, or short stress relief breaks?
3. **Modify Your Environment**: Remove triggers or rearrange your living or workspace to better support your goals.
4. **Seek Expert Guidance**: If you feel stuck, talk to a counselor, career advisor, or someone experienced in the area you are struggling with.

Using new approaches can prevent repeated stumbles over the same problem.

17.11 Handling Disappointment in Others

Sometimes you feel let down by friends or family who do not keep their word or who fail to understand your needs:

- **Communicate Clearly**: Make sure they truly understand your expectations. Sometimes, unmet expectations happen due to miscommunication.

- **Reevaluate Your Assumptions**: Perhaps you assumed they had the same priorities or resources that you do.
- **Set Boundaries if Needed**: If someone repeatedly fails you or disrespects your recovery, limit how much you rely on them.
- **Offer Second Chances Wisely**: People can learn and grow, but if the same hurtful pattern repeats many times, it may be best to step away or lower your expectations of that person.

Being honest about your feelings and adjusting your reliance on others can spare you repeated heartbreak.

17.12 Dealing with a Series of Setbacks (Piling On)

Sometimes, problems come in groups—job loss, health scare, relationship trouble—all at once. This can feel overwhelming:

1. **Prioritize**: Identify the most urgent matter (e.g., health first, then finances). Tackle them in order instead of trying to solve everything simultaneously.
2. **Ask for Help**: Family, friends, support groups, or professionals can share the load. You do not have to handle multiple crises alone.
3. **Maintain Basic Routines**: Even if life is chaotic, try to keep sleeping, eating, and short relaxation times consistent. This ensures you have enough energy to cope.
4. **Reward Small Achievements**: If you solve even one part of the pile, acknowledge your effort. Recognizing progress boosts morale.
5. **Stay Flexible**: Unexpected changes may force you to adjust your plan. Try not to see this as failure, just a necessary shift.

Approaching multiple setbacks methodically can help you avoid total burnout.

17.13 Less-Known Ways to Deal with Disappointment

Below are some creative tips that might not be in basic self-help guides:

1. **"If/Then" Scripts**: Write out possible problems ("If I get turned down for this job...") and list a "Then" plan ("Then I'll call my friend for advice and apply to three more listings tomorrow."). Having these scripts can reduce panic when something goes wrong.
2. **Thought Write-Down**: When disappointed, quickly jot down the thought swirling in your mind, then write a calmer answer next to it. For instance, "I can't trust anyone" → "I need to communicate better or find more reliable people."
3. **Mini-Closure Ritual**: If you fail at a goal, do a small act to mark the end, like discarding old notes or reorganizing your workspace. This can mentally free you to move forward rather than cling to the defeat.

These small techniques can shift your mindset from despair to productive thinking.

17.14 Restoring Self-Belief After a Big Letdown

If your setback was large—like a relapse that lasted weeks or a major work project failure—you might wonder if you can ever recover:

- **Gather Evidence of Past Wins**: Make a short list of achievements. Remember the times you overcame big obstacles.
- **Talk to Someone Who Believes in You**: Their confidence can spark your own. Hearing them say, "I know you can bounce back," is powerful.
- **Take One Bold Step**: Do something that shows yourself you can still act effectively, even if small, like applying for a new position or revisiting a daily recovery routine.
- **Visual Reminders**: Place encouraging words or images where you see them each day (like on your mirror or phone lock screen).

Rebuilding self-belief is a process. Consistent, small actions can piece your confidence back together.

17.15 Using Humor to Ease the Pain of Disappointment

Laughter does not magically solve problems, but it can reduce stress and give fresh perspectives:

- **Safe Comedy**: Watch a stand-up routine, a funny show, or read jokes you find healthy and not triggering.
- **Laugh with a Friend**: Call someone who understands your humor. Sharing a light moment can break the tension.
- **Laugh at Minor Mistakes**: If the setback is small or fixable, seeing the silly side can lessen its emotional weight.

Humor should not be used to avoid serious matters, but it can release some pressure so you think more clearly.

17.16 Knowing When to Let Go of a Goal

Some disappointments signal that a certain path is no longer right for you:

- **Honest Assessment**: Are you chasing a goal that conflicts with your current values or puts you in risky surroundings?
- **Cost vs. Benefit**: Is this pursuit causing more harm than good to your mental health, finances, or relationships?
- **Talk to Mentors**: Get input from people you trust. Maybe a pivot or a new approach is better.
- **No Shame in Changing Plans**: Abandoning a misguided goal can free your energy for something more suitable.

Letting go is different from giving up out of fear. It is about recognizing a path that no longer aligns with your recovery or well-being.

17.17 Preventing Disappointment from Hardening Your Heart

Sometimes, repeated setbacks can make people numb or cynical. They decide it is "safer not to care." But shutting down can lead to loneliness and missed opportunities:

- **Stay Open to Hope**: Even after pain, new successes or friendships are possible. Letting bitterness take over can block those chances.
- **Focus on Realistic Optimism**: You can hope for good outcomes while being prepared for difficulties.
- **Limit Harmful Media or Conversations**: Constant exposure to doom-and-gloom news or negative talk can fuel cynicism. Balance it with uplifting stories or positive influences.
- **Practice Gratitude**: Even in a rough period, noticing small good things—a helpful coworker, a warm meal—can keep you from sinking into total negativity.

Protecting your openness helps you continue growing, learning, and connecting with others in a healthy way.

17.18 Key Points from Chapter 17

1. Setbacks can arise from stress overload, lack of support, sudden events, or growing overconfidence. They do not mean total failure.
2. A quick response to a slip can prevent it from escalating. Pausing, admitting the mistake, and seeking support are early steps.
3. Disappointment triggers strong emotions like guilt, anger, or shame, but these feelings can be managed with honest reflection and discussion.
4. Separate the event from your self-worth to keep your sense of competence intact.
5. If you slip back into old harmful habits, halt immediately, remove triggers, and update your prevention plan.
6. Turning disappointment into insight means asking, "What can I learn here?" and adjusting your approach.
7. Balance self-blame with recognition of external factors to avoid getting stuck in guilt or denial.
8. Face others' disappointment calmly: listen, apologize if necessary, and show how you will improve.
9. Emotional resilience can be built through daily self-care, positive self-talk, stable support systems, and incremental goals.
10. A series of setbacks can feel overwhelming; prioritize tasks, ask for help, and keep core routines.

11. Less-known tips like "If/Then" scripts, short write-downs, or mini-closure rituals can move you past disappointment.
12. Restore self-belief after a big letdown by recalling past wins, seeking encouragement, and taking small, bold steps forward.
13. Humor can ease the sting of failure but should not replace genuine problem-solving.
14. Sometimes letting go of a goal is wise if it no longer aligns with your well-being or values.
15. Protect yourself from becoming numb or cynical. Staying open to realistic optimism keeps you engaged in life and growth.

Conclusion

Disappointment and setbacks are normal parts of life, especially when rebuilding after an addictive habit. Though they can feel crushing, they also offer chances to improve coping skills, refine your plans, and deepen your self-knowledge. The key is to face the letdown head-on: admit what happened, seek help, and adjust your methods. By viewing each slip as a challenge rather than a final defeat, you keep moving forward on your healthier path.

In the next chapter, we will focus on long-term care of your body and mind (Chapter 18). This will include ways to stay physically well, maintain emotional balance over the years, and plan for a future that supports ongoing mental health. Dealing with setbacks is easier when your overall health is strong, so building robust self-care habits can be a protective layer against future stumbles.

CHAPTER 18: KEEPING A HEALTHY BODY AND MIND OVER TIME

Introduction
Your body and mind are closely linked. When one suffers, the other often does too. After working through the initial challenges of leaving a harmful habit, the next step is to develop habits that help you remain stable and strong for years to come. Caring for both your physical and mental health is an ongoing process that goes beyond avoiding old behaviors. It involves nutrition, exercise, stress management, checkups, and plenty of nurturing practices that make life richer and more stable.

This chapter explores how to protect and support your body as you continue on a healthier path, as well as how to maintain emotional balance over the long haul. You will read about scheduling regular appointments, simple exercise and food choices, mental renewal, and ways to keep stress from building up. By building a solid foundation of daily care, you strengthen your defenses against relapse, burnout, and other risks. A well-cared-for body and mind can sustain your progress and help you embrace the positives of living free from harmful habits.

18.1 Why Ongoing Care Matters

Many people focus on short-term fixes right after quitting a harmful behavior. However, your body and mind need consistent attention:

- **Preventing Relapse**: Good physical health and mental balance can lower craving intensity and make you more resilient.
- **Boosting Mood**: A well-nourished body and balanced mind often produce more stable emotions and clearer thoughts.
- **Supporting Daily Life**: Tasks like working, studying, or caring for family become less stressful when you feel physically energized and mentally steady.
- **Longevity and Quality of Life**: Building healthy habits now can protect you from chronic diseases and mental health decline later.

Instead of seeing health as a one-time goal, view it as an ongoing lifestyle that supports everything else you do.

18.2 Setting Up a Basic Health Routine

A daily routine that cares for your body does not have to be complicated:

1. **Consistent Wake-Up and Bedtime**: Aim for around 7-9 hours of sleep if possible. Going to bed and rising at the same time daily stabilizes your internal clock.
2. **Hydration**: Drink water regularly. Dehydration can worsen mood swings and fatigue.
3. **Balanced Meals**: Include protein, vegetables, fruits, and whole grains. If you can, reduce sugary snacks and highly processed foods.
4. **Light Exercise**: Aim for at least 15-30 minutes of movement each day, whether it is a walk, home workout, or gentle stretching.
5. **Short Stress Breaks**: Throughout the day, pause to breathe deeply, stretch, or rest your eyes from screens.

These small actions, done regularly, make a big difference over time.

18.3 Staying Active in a Manageable Way

Exercise does not require a gym membership or intense regimes. The key is consistency:

- **Find Something You Like**: If you dislike running, do not force it. Try dancing, low-impact aerobics, or brisk walks.
- **Sneak in Movement**: Take the stairs, park farther away, or do simple stretches during breaks.
- **Set Realistic Goals**: Start with short sessions and build up. Ten minutes of daily movement can still have benefits.
- **Listen to Your Body**: If you experience pain or feel dizzy, slow down or consult a professional. Overdoing it can lead to injury or discouragement.
- **Invite a Friend**: Doing activities with someone can be fun and keeps you accountable.

Being active boosts your body's strength, improves circulation, and can release mood-lifting chemicals in the brain.

18.4 Healthy Eating without Strict Rules

Strict diets can backfire by creating stress or guilt. Instead, aim for balanced meals:

- **Focus on Whole Foods**: Try to include fruits, vegetables, whole grains, lean proteins, and healthy fats.
- **Watch Portion Sizes**: Eating mindfully, noticing when you are satisfied rather than stuffed.
- **Limit Sugary Drinks**: Sodas or energy drinks can spike your energy briefly but lead to crashes and health issues if consumed in excess.
- **Snack Smart**: Swap chips or candy for nuts, seeds, yogurt, or fresh fruit if you can.
- **Stay Flexible**: Allow occasional treats. Complete restriction can fuel unhealthy cravings or binge behaviors.

Eating well supports brain function, mood stability, and the energy you need to maintain your recovery plan.

18.5 Scheduling Checkups and Screening

Regular doctor visits can catch small problems before they grow:

- **Annual Physicals**: Check vital signs, blood tests, or talk about any concerns with a medical professional.
- **Dental Care**: Your oral health can affect your overall health. Aim for regular cleanings and checkups if possible.
- **Mental Health Check-Ins**: Even if you feel okay, periodic talks with a counselor or support group can catch small emotional struggles.
- **Vision and Hearing**: Many people ignore eye and ear care. If you notice changes, do not wait—get it checked.

- **Follow Medication Plans**: If you are on medicine for anxiety, depression, or any condition, follow the schedule and let your doctor know if you have side effects or new symptoms.

Consistent checkups help you manage long-term conditions and maintain your physical well-being so that health issues do not undermine your progress.

18.6 Creating a Calm Living Environment

Your surroundings at home can either raise or lower daily stress. A calmer environment supports mental health:

1. **Tidy Up**: Clutter can add mental pressure. A simple, organized space feels more peaceful.
2. **Fresh Air**: If possible, open windows or use a fan to keep air moving. Stale air can affect mood and alertness.
3. **Soothing Decor**: Soft lighting, a few plants, or colors you find relaxing can make a big difference.
4. **Noise Control**: If you share a space, consider headphones for quiet music or white noise to block distractions.
5. **Personal Touches**: Pictures of loved ones, small items that remind you of happy moments, or motivational notes can keep your spirits up.

A supportive home environment helps you recharge, improving both your physical and mental balance.

18.7 Managing Stress Over the Long Haul

Stress is part of life, but unchecked stress can harm your body and mind. These tips can help:

- **Plan Breaks**: Short mental rest periods throughout the day prevent stress overload.
- **Use Relaxation Techniques**: Such as gentle stretches, progressive muscle relaxation, or guided breathing apps.

- **Organize Tasks**: Making to-do lists and prioritizing can keep you from feeling overwhelmed.
- **Build a Stress-Relief Kit**: Include items like a stress ball, soothing music, a journal, or a comforting drink.
- **Learn to Say "No"**: Do not overcommit. Protect your schedule so you have downtime to recharge.

Managing stress daily prevents it from piling up into bigger emotional or physical issues later.

18.8 Maintaining Emotional Wellness

Mental well-being goes beyond avoiding depression or anxiety; it also means feeling purposeful and at ease. Consider:

- **Daily Reflection**: Write or think about one positive aspect of your day, or one act of kindness you noticed.
- **Emotional Check-Ins**: Ask yourself, "How am I feeling right now?" Recognizing emotions early can keep them from boiling over.
- **Healthy Outlets for Feelings**: Painting, music, talking to a friend, or spending time in nature can all reduce inner tension.
- **Mindfulness or Meditative Moments**: Even one minute of paying attention to your breath can ground you.
- **Realistic Self-Talk**: Practice saying, "I can handle this step by step," rather than, "Everything is going wrong."

Supporting emotional wellness makes it easier to stay committed to long-term health goals.

18.9 Balancing Work, Family, and Personal Time

Continuing from Chapter 13, keep the balance going in the long term:

- **Revisit Your Schedule Often**: As life changes—new jobs, evolving relationships—adapt your time blocks.

- **Set Boundaries at Work**: If possible, avoid letting job demands seep into all your evenings or weekends.
- **Regular Family Meetings**: Discuss chores, schedules, or conflicts before they grow. Keep the atmosphere calm and solution-focused.
- **Schedule Personal Time**: Even if it is 10–15 minutes each day to read, stretch, or enjoy a hobby.
- **Stay Flexible**: If stress rises in one area, temporarily reduce demands in another. Seek help when you feel overwhelmed.

Balance is a moving target. Checking in regularly helps you adjust and maintain stability.

18.10 Finding Long-Term Motivation

Staying healthy is not always exciting, and motivation can dip. Here are ways to keep going:

1. **Set Fun Challenges**: Like trying a new healthy recipe each week or learning a simple physical skill (such as light yoga poses).
2. **Track Progress**: Keep a basic log of steps, workouts, or mood improvements. Seeing progress over time can remind you why you are doing this.
3. **Reward Yourself**: Use safe, modest treats—like a relaxing bath or a new book—when you hit small milestones (for example, exercising consistently for a month).
4. **Visualize the Benefits**: Remember how it felt to be stuck in old harmful habits. Reflect on how much better life is now that you are healthier.

Motivation ebbs and flows, but small incentives and positive reminders keep you on the path.

18.11 Handling Relapses in Health Habits

Even well-meaning health goals can slip. You might skip workouts, eat poorly for a while, or neglect rest:

- **Recognize Quickly**: Notice when you have gone off track. Maybe your energy is lower, or you see weight changes, or your mood drops.
- **Adjust Gently**: Return to simpler routines rather than punishing yourself with extreme measures.
- **Seek Accountability**: Tell a friend or partner, "I want to get back on track. Can we check in daily?"
- **Pinpoint the Cause**: Was it boredom, stress, or scheduling issues? Fixing the root cause makes your routine more sustainable.
- **Emphasize Learning**: A slip can teach you which parts of your routine are fragile and need extra attention.

Remember, occasional slips do not mean you must give up on healthy living altogether. Correcting a slip early helps you avoid bigger setbacks.

18.12 Long-Term Support for Your Health

It helps to have people and resources that keep you on the right track year after year:

- **Regular Appointments**: Staying in touch with a mental health professional or a supportive doctor can keep small issues from growing.
- **Join Activity Groups**: Whether it is a walking club, a sports league, or an art circle, being around others with similar interests can keep you engaged.
- **Stay in Recovery Groups**: If you found a good recovery community, consider staying involved even if you feel strong. Your experiences can help newcomers and keep you motivated.
- **Online Communities**: Follow fitness or mental health channels that share tips and encouragement if you enjoy social media in a balanced way.

Constant engagement with helpful networks makes healthy living feel normal rather than forced.

18.13 Protecting Your Sleep

Sleep is a cornerstone of both physical and mental health:

1. **Wind-Down Routine**: Dim lights, lower screen brightness, or read something calming before bed. Avoid stimulating activities right before sleep.
2. **Steady Schedule**: Going to bed and rising at a similar time daily can improve sleep quality.
3. **Limit Caffeine and Heavy Meals**: Especially in the evening, as they can delay or disrupt sleep.
4. **Silent or Dark Room**: If noise is an issue, use earplugs or white noise. If light is an issue, consider an eye mask or blackout curtains.
5. **Watch for Sleep Disorders**: If you consistently wake up tired or snore loudly, talk to a doctor. Conditions like sleep apnea can sabotage rest.

A well-rested brain is better at handling cravings, stress, and emotional ups and downs.

18.14 Ongoing Stress-Reduction Habits

Stress can creep back in if you let your guard down. Keep a toolbox of habits for daily life:

- **Relaxing Music or Sounds**: Listening to gentle music, nature sounds, or guided relaxation can calm nerves.
- **Light Journaling**: Note daily worries or achievements. Offloading thoughts can reduce nighttime anxiety.
- **Practice Kindness**: Doing small kind acts for others can raise your mood and reduce stress.
- **Short Nature Visits**: If available, a quick walk in a park or by water can refresh your mind and lower tension.
- **Breathing Apps or Exercises**: Guided breathing sessions can be done anywhere and help center you quickly.

Returning to these habits each day prevents stress from piling up to harmful levels.

18.15 Less-Known Tips for Body and Mind Care

Below are some unique ideas to enrich your routine:

1. **Micro-Workouts**: Do very short bursts of exercise throughout the day—like squats during TV commercials or 5-minute yoga stretches every hour.
2. **Meal Prep Sundays**: If you have time, cook in batches and freeze portions to avoid daily stress about "What's for dinner?"
3. **Body Scan Breaks**: Once or twice a day, close your eyes and mentally scan for tension in your muscles, releasing tight spots as you notice them.
4. **Sunlight Moments**: Natural light can boost mood and help regulate body rhythms. Step outside for a few minutes when possible.
5. **Set Alarms for Activity**: If your job is sedentary, a gentle reminder on your phone every hour can prompt you to stand and stretch.

These small methods can fit into busy lives and create layers of self-care.

18.16 Planning for Bigger Life Changes

Over the years, you might face major transitions—moving to a new city, changing jobs, starting or ending relationships:

- **Map Out Supports**: Before a big shift, identify resources (like local counselors in the new area or a close friend who can offer phone support).
- **Continue Key Routines**: Keep parts of your normal routine (like morning stretches or evening reflection) to maintain a sense of stability.
- **Ask for Advice**: Speak with mentors or peers who went through similar changes.
- **Stay Aware of Old Urges**: Times of major change can trigger the desire to slip back into harmful habits. Stay prepared with a plan if cravings flare up.

Thinking ahead about major life changes protects you from losing the healthy base you have built.

18.17 Giving Back and Feeling Fulfilled

Maintaining a healthier mind and body can also include contributing to causes or communities that matter to you:

- **Volunteering**: Helping others can reinforce your own sense of purpose. It might be in an animal shelter, a food bank, or a community event.
- **Peer Support**: If you feel secure in your recovery, consider mentoring someone who is newer to the process. Sharing your lessons can solidify your own growth.
- **Creative Expression**: Activities like writing, painting, or playing music for a community can channel your energy in a positive way.
- **Community Projects**: Clean-up drives, local sports, or neighborhood improvement tasks link you to others and remind you that you have something valuable to offer.

Contributing to the well-being of others can also strengthen your commitment to staying healthy.

18.18 Key Points from Chapter 18

1. Long-term health care is a daily effort, not a one-time fix, and it helps prevent relapse and protects mental well-being.
2. A basic routine includes consistent sleep, balanced meals, regular hydration, light exercise, and short stress breaks.
3. Consistent checkups (physical, dental, mental) catch problems early and keep you informed about your health.
4. Craft a calm living environment with simple organization, fresh air, soothing decor, and personal touches.
5. Stress management is ongoing; practice small daily tactics like breathing exercises and organized task lists.
6. Emotional wellness involves daily check-ins, realistic self-talk, and outlets for feelings (like art, journaling, or nature).
7. Maintaining work–life balance requires periodic adjustments and boundary-setting.
8. Keep motivation high with fun challenges, progress tracking, safe rewards, and remembering the benefits of healthy living.

9. If you slip up on health goals, correct it early, figure out why it happened, and ease back into your routine.
10. Seek and maintain support from medical professionals, activity groups, or online communities.
11. Good sleep habits are crucial for mood and energy; create a bedtime routine and guard your rest.
12. Extra ideas like micro-workouts, meal prep, body scans, or sun breaks can boost your overall care.
13. Plan ahead for big life changes to prevent them from disturbing your mental and physical balance.
14. Contributing to others' well-being can enrich your own sense of purpose and keep you focused on staying healthy.

Conclusion
Keeping a healthy body and mind over time calls for sustained attention, but the rewards are significant. By following simple daily routines, staying alert to warning signs, and adjusting your plan as life changes, you create a solid base for ongoing stability. Physical well-being underpins mental resilience, which in turn reduces the lure of old harmful habits. Whether you are months or years into recovery, investing in your physical and emotional health remains an essential part of protecting your progress.

In the upcoming chapters, we will look at building trust, hope, and healthy future plans (Chapter 19) and then moving forward with inner strength (Chapter 20). With your mind and body in good shape, you can look ahead with greater confidence. Your energy can then flow into the goals and connections that bring you fulfillment, creating a more peaceful and rewarding life after addiction.

CHAPTER 19: TRUST, HOPE, AND HEALTHY PLANS

Introduction

Once you have set up routines for physical and mental well-being (see Chapter 18), you are in a stronger position to think about trust, hope, and how to shape your future plans. Trust may have been broken in your relationships during the time you were using harmful habits, or you may still feel uneasy trusting yourself after past lapses. Meanwhile, hope can feel shaky if you are worried that old patterns might return or that life will throw new obstacles in your path. In this chapter, we will look at rebuilding trust (both with yourself and with others), fostering hope in a genuine way, and creating healthy plans that can guide you forward without adding extra stress.

Building trust can take time and effort, especially if past actions caused harm or led others to doubt your promises. Hope is often connected to trust—if you do not trust yourself to follow through, hope can feel weak. The good news is that every small, consistent step you take can strengthen both trust and hope. By combining honesty, practical actions, and a flexible plan for the future, you can steadily restore faith in your own growth and show others that they can rely on you as well.

19.1 Rebuilding Self-Trust

Why Self-Trust Matters

Self-trust is the foundation of your confidence. If you doubt your ability to keep promises or manage cravings, it can create a cycle of anxiety. On the other hand, when you believe in your own reliability, you are less likely to be swayed by negative thoughts or external pressure.

Practical Ways to Restore Self-Trust

1. **Keep Small Promises to Yourself**: Start with tasks you know you can handle, like making your bed daily or drinking a glass of water when you wake up. Each time you follow through, you prove to yourself that you can do what you say.

2. **Write a Personal Code**: Note a few simple principles that guide your behavior—like treating people kindly or being honest in your words. Review them often.
3. **Admit Mistakes Quickly**: When you stumble or realize you forgot something, acknowledge it. Hiding or denying slips can erode trust in yourself.
4. **Track Your Wins**: If you have a small notebook or phone app, list at least one success daily. This can be as simple as resisting a craving, calming yourself down instead of exploding, or completing a short exercise session.

Self-trust grows through consistent action, honesty, and patience. Over time, you will feel more stable and less likely to sabotage your progress.

19.2 Repairing Trust with Others

Understanding Broken Trust
Hurtful behaviors from the past—like lying to cover an addiction, not showing up for important events, or breaking promises—can damage relationships. Others might worry that you will revert to old habits, or they might fear your words are empty.

Methods to Rebuild Trust in Relationships

1. **Open Communication**: Be clear about what you are doing to stay healthy. For example, share that you are attending meetings, exercising daily, or following a new routine. This transparency helps people see real change.
2. **Consistency Over Words**: Grand statements or apologies can sound good, but consistent follow-through is what convinces people. If you say you will call at a certain time, do it. If you promise to pay back borrowed money, do it in a timely manner.
3. **Patience with Skepticism**: Some family or friends may not trust you right away, even if you have been clean or stable for months. They might be waiting to see if your behavior truly sticks. Avoid pressuring them to forgive or forget immediately.

4. **Show Respect for Their Feelings**: If someone is still angry or sad about past hurts, let them express it. Then calmly share how you understand their point of view and outline your commitment to do better.

Over time, reliable actions usually speak louder than promises. Keep in mind that some relationships might need professional help, like family counseling, if the hurt runs very deep.

19.3 Recognizing Genuine Hope Versus Wishful Thinking

Why Hope Matters
Hope can keep you going when challenges rise. It can give you the energy to try new approaches or stay with healthy habits despite boredom or setbacks. However, hope must be grounded in realistic ideas. False hope—where you ignore real risks—can lead to sudden disappointment.

Realistic Hope Building

1. **Base It on Evidence**: Look back at moments when you handled stress well or overcame a crisis. Use those memories as proof that you can succeed again.
2. **Look for Role Models**: Spot people who have stayed healthy for years after addiction. Note their methods. Seeing their success can fuel genuine hope.
3. **Plan for Obstacles**: Hope is stronger when you acknowledge potential hurdles and have a "What if?" plan. For example, "If I feel a craving during a stressful workday, I will reach out to my sponsor or do a breathing exercise in a quiet corner."
4. **Keep a Forward Focus**: While it is good to learn from the past, do not dwell there. Hope looks ahead. You might say, "I have learned from those mistakes, and now I am making a steady plan to avoid repeating them."

Balanced hope does not ignore problems; it accepts them and prepares for them while still believing in your ability to move in a healthier direction.

19.4 Creating Healthy Plans for the Future

Why Planning Helps
Having a plan gives you a sense of direction. It can reduce anxiety by showing you which steps to take next, whether in career, education, relationships, or personal development. However, plans should be flexible enough to handle unexpected changes.

Steps to Form a Plan

1. **Define Your Aim**: Be specific but realistic. For instance, "I want to complete a certain training program in the next six months," or "I want to save a certain amount of money over the next year."
2. **List Actionable Tasks**: Break each aim into small steps. For example, if you want a new job, steps might include updating your resume, asking a friend to proofread it, applying to three positions a week, and practicing interview skills.
3. **Set Milestones**: Mark points in your timeline to check your progress. For example, "By next month, I will have applied to at least eight companies."
4. **Schedule Regular Reviews**: Once or twice a month, review how your plan is going. Adjust if you are off track or if new opportunities arise.

Remember not to overload yourself with too many big plans at once. Pick one or two main goals so you can focus your energy and avoid feeling swamped.

19.5 Balancing Ambition and Self-Care

When you start feeling better, you might want to make up for lost time—perhaps you want a promotion at work, to rebuild every broken relationship quickly, or to handle multiple big projects at once. While ambition can be healthy, it can also lead to burnout if you ignore self-care.

Tips for Keeping Ambition Balanced

1. **Stay Attuned to Stress Signs**: If your body shows signs of tension (headaches, insomnia, irritability), step back and evaluate your schedule.

2. **Avoid Perfectionism**: Trying to do everything perfectly is a common trap. Accept that some tasks can be done "well enough" if it means protecting your well-being.
3. **Schedule Recovery Time**: Whether it is a weekend day without major commitments or a nightly break, you need pockets of rest in your routine.
4. **Stay in Touch with Your Supporters**: If you find yourself drifting from your recovery group or ignoring therapy sessions, that might be a sign you are pushing too hard in other areas of life.

A balanced approach to your goals can keep you climbing steadily without risking a big crash.

19.6 Overcoming Doubt and Setbacks in Planning

Even with the best plan, you might run into doubt or external problems. The key is to adjust rather than abandon the entire idea.

Common Obstacles

- **Lack of Immediate Results**: You might think, "I have tried for a month, and nothing changed." Real progress often comes with time.
- **Unexpected Life Events**: Job layoffs, family issues, or health crises can force you to pause or revise your plan.
- **Inner Voices of Fear**: Thoughts like, "I am not good enough," or "I might fail anyway," can freeze you if you let them.

How to Keep Moving

1. **Refine the Plan**: If a step is too big, break it further. If a method is not working, try another.
2. **Seek Advice**: Talk to a mentor, counselor, or a trusted friend who can see the situation from a different angle.
3. **Remember Past Wins**: Reflect on moments when you overcame something similar. Use that memory as evidence that you can adapt now too.

Flexibility is crucial. Changing your approach is not the same as giving up.

19.7 Handling Pressure from Others

Sometimes family or friends expect quick results. They might say, "When will you finish that degree?" or "You should have a better job by now." Although they may mean well, such comments can feel like extra weight on your shoulders.

Strategies for Dealing with Pressure

1. **Communicate Your Reality**: Calmly explain your plan and your reasons for moving at a certain pace. For instance, "I need to keep my daily recovery routine, so I cannot take extra overtime right now."
2. **Set Firm Boundaries**: If they constantly push you in ways that feel unhealthy, let them know you appreciate their concern but must do what works for you.
3. **Focus on Your Goals**: Remind yourself of the value of your method. You are the one living your life, and you understand your recovery needs best.
4. **Ask for Support Instead**: Sometimes, people want to help but do not know how. Suggest ways they can genuinely support you—like offering a ride to an interview or helping with a chore while you study.

Sticking to your well-thought-out plan is often better than letting others rush you into choices you are not ready for.

19.8 Finding Hope in Small Daily Moments

While aiming for big changes is good, day-to-day life also offers moments of satisfaction or hope. Noticing them can keep your mood lifted.

Ideas to Spot Hope in the Ordinary

1. **Micro-Achievements**: Finished a small task on your to-do list, prepared a healthy meal, or resisted a minor urge? Congratulate yourself. These tiny steps matter.
2. **Nature's Calm**: Watching a sunset, feeling a breeze, or listening to birds can remind you that there is more to life than stress or worry.
3. **Kindness from Others**: If someone holds a door for you, offers a friendly smile, or says a supportive word, let it reaffirm that good things still exist around you.

4. **Personal Joy**: A favorite song, a short funny video, or a chat with a close friend can give you a quick mood boost.

Recognizing these small signs of positivity each day can build a consistent sense of hope and stability.

19.9 Realigning When Your Plans Evolve

Your dreams and goals might shift over time. Maybe you discover a new interest or realize a certain path is not as fulfilling as you once thought. Changing plans does not mean you have failed; it can mean you are maturing and learning more about yourself.

How to Handle Shifts

1. **Pause and Reflect**: Ask why you want to change direction. Are you avoiding a challenge out of fear, or are you honestly finding a better fit?
2. **Talk It Through**: Share your thoughts with a mentor or loved one. They might offer insight you have not considered.
3. **Transition Thoughtfully**: Do not drop everything in haste. If possible, leave a job or path responsibly, making sure you have at least a basic safety net in place.
4. **Keep Core Healthy Habits**: Even if you switch careers or relocate, stick to the daily routines that support your recovery—like regular sleep, exercise, or group check-ins.

Adapting your plan can keep you aligned with your real interests and values as you grow more secure in your healthier life.

19.10 The Connection Between Trust, Hope, and Plans

Trust, hope, and planning form a loop:

- **Trust** builds as you fulfill small goals, showing yourself and others you can be reliable.

- **Hope** grows when you see that progress is possible, especially if you have a steady plan to keep building on.
- **Healthy Plans** are easier to follow when you trust yourself to do them and believe (hope) that they matter.

When one of these elements weakens, the other two can help you strengthen it again. For instance, if your hope dips, you might rely on trust in your well-designed routine or recall how far you have already come (which can spark new hope).

19.11 Less-Known Tips for Sustaining Hope and Trust

Below are some ideas that might not appear in typical guides:

1. **"Anchor Objects"**: Keep a small object (like a coin, a pebble, or a simple bracelet) that symbolizes your promise to stay committed. Each time you see or touch it, recall the trust you are building.
2. **Future-Self Letters**: Write a short note to yourself about what you hope to see in six months. Put the letter away. When that time arrives, read it to see how your real outcomes match your hopes.
3. **Visual Timelines**: Draw a simple timeline from your past to your near future. Mark past achievements and future aims. Seeing it visually can make your path more tangible.
4. **"If I Don't, Then..."**: Sometimes we focus on what will happen if we succeed but forget the cost of giving up. Listing the negative outcomes if you abandon your plan can fuel motivation to push through tough times.

These small, creative tools can anchor your progress and remind you why you are working so diligently on trust and hope.

19.12 Handling Fear of Success

Oddly enough, fear of success can appear when you start doing well. You might worry that more will be expected of you or that people will judge you if you slip.

- **Recognize It**: If you find yourself sabotaging your progress, ask whether you are afraid of being seen as "fully recovered" or more responsible.

- **Level the Expectations**: Understand that success does not mean you must be perfect. You can continue to have human flaws while moving forward.
- **Seek Reassurance**: Talk to a mentor or counselor about these fears. Knowing that others have felt the same way can ease your mind.
- **Remember Your Purpose**: You chose healthier habits for a reason—improving your life, feeling better each day, and respecting those around you. Focus on those benefits rather than the fear of extra pressure.

Accept that success will bring new challenges, but it also brings many rewards that can far outweigh those worries.

19.13 Trust and Hope in Groups or Communities

If you are part of a support group, place of worship, or community center, you have even more opportunities to grow trust and hope:

- **Shared Experience**: Hearing stories from others who overcame similar issues can reinforce your belief that progress is real.
- **Public Commitments**: Telling your group about your aims can strengthen your commitment, because now you have caring witnesses.
- **Giving and Receiving Support**: Trust deepens when you both offer help and accept it graciously from others.
- **Events and Milestones**: Community gatherings, skill-building workshops, or group challenges can give you new goals and fresh energy.

Cautiously choose groups that align with your goals and values, so you do not encounter negative influences that undermine trust or hope.

19.14 Reaffirming Your "Why"

When hope feels low or trust is shaky, revisit your original reasons for choosing a healthier life.

- **List the Gains**: Improved relationships, better health, more stable emotions, fewer legal or financial problems, and a clearer conscience.

- **Remember the Pain**: Recalling how bad things got can motivate you not to return there.
- **Envision the Future**: Picture the peace and possibilities that come from staying on track. Maybe you see yourself in a stable home, with a satisfying job, or enjoying calm weekends without the burden of addiction.

Reminding yourself of your "why" can refocus your mind and boost your resolve to stay on the healthy path.

19.15 Checking In Regularly

Trust, hope, and plans are not "set it and forget it" elements. They need nurturing.

- **Weekly Self-Check**: Ask, "Do I trust myself more or less than last week? What events influenced that?"
- **Monthly Review**: Look at your goals, see what progress you made, and note any changes needed.
- **Share in a Support Group**: If you attend weekly or monthly meetings, mention your progress or doubts. Others may have useful advice.
- **Adjust as Needed**: If you see a consistent dip in your hope or trust levels, it might signal you need more support, a simpler goal, or a talk with a professional.

Treat these check-ins as routine maintenance for your mental and emotional well-being.

19.16 Success is a Process, Not a One-Time Finish

It is easy to assume that trust and hope will be fully repaired once you hit a milestone—like being a year free of harmful habits or mending one major relationship. But real growth continues beyond these milestones.

Long-Term Perspective

1. **Expect Ongoing Learning**: Life events, changes in your circle, or stress at work can reveal new vulnerabilities. Stay curious and proactive.

2. **Celebrate Steps Along the Way**: Each level of improvement deserves recognition.
3. **Keep Building Skills**: Communication skills, conflict resolution, and emotional regulation can deepen and refine over time, helping you keep trust strong.
4. **Adapt to Aging and Life Shifts**: As you get older, your body and priorities might change. What worked when you were 30 might differ at 50. Stay open to evolving your strategies.

By viewing success as a process, you avoid the disappointment of thinking you should be "done" at any point. Growth can be lifelong, and that is okay.

19.17 Less-Known Ideas for Strengthening Trust and Hope Daily

1. **Affirmation Swap**: Pair up with a friend and each day send one supportive, honest affirmation about your progress. It helps both of you.
2. **Photo or Audio Diary**: Quickly snap a picture of something good each day or record a short voice note about a positive moment. Reviewing them can refresh your trust and hope.
3. **Create a "Hope Board"**: Pin or tape encouraging quotes, small achievements, and pictures that represent your future aims. Keep it somewhere you see frequently.
4. **Silent Reflection**: Take 2–5 minutes in complete quiet at some point in the day, focusing on any feeling of gratitude or peace that arises.

Such habits sprinkle daily reminders of your capacity to trust yourself and aim for a better tomorrow.

19.18 Key Points from Chapter 19

1. Restoring self-trust starts with keeping small promises, tracking wins, and being honest about mistakes.
2. Repairing trust in relationships requires open communication, consistent behavior, and patience with skepticism from others.
3. Genuine hope is based on realistic views of obstacles, evidence of past success, and role models of long-term stability.

4. Healthy plans involve clear goals, step-by-step actions, and regular check-ins to adjust as life changes.
5. Balancing ambition with self-care prevents burnout and protects the progress you have already made.
6. When plans face setbacks, be flexible: refine steps, seek advice, and remember past wins to keep moving forward.
7. Pressures from others should be addressed by explaining your reality, setting boundaries, and focusing on your own well-being.
8. Look for small daily moments of positivity to maintain hope, such as micro-achievements, simple pleasures, and kind gestures.
9. Plans may shift over time. Changing course is not a failure but often a sign of growth and self-awareness.
10. Trust, hope, and planning form a loop—each one supports the others.
11. Fear of success can happen. Recognize it, manage it by speaking honestly, and keep your benefits in view.
12. Community or group involvement can reinforce hope through shared experiences and mutual support.
13. Revisit your "why" whenever hope or trust falters, recalling both the benefits of your new life and the pain of the old.
14. Regular check-ins keep trust and hope strong by highlighting where you are thriving or need more help.
15. Success is an ongoing path. Even after major milestones, staying attentive to your mental and emotional growth remains key.

Conclusion

Trust and hope are like pillars that support the healthier life you are building. As you develop meaningful plans and follow through with daily steps, both pillars gain strength. Even if trust was badly broken in the past—whether in yourself or with others—you can rebuild it by showing consistent, honest actions over time. Hope, too, is nourished when you see small improvements, adapt to challenges, and keep an eye on future possibilities.

In the final chapter (Chapter 20), we will discuss the concept of moving forward with inner strength. You will read about how to keep thriving and maintaining what you have built—using all the tools and insights from this book. By Chapter 20's end, you should feel equipped with a wide range of methods to sustain your mental health and personal growth after addiction. Your story continues from there, backed by the trust you have rebuilt, the hope you have discovered, and the healthy plans you have set in motion.

CHAPTER 20: MOVING FORWARD WITH INNER STRENGTH

Introduction
As you reach this final chapter, you have explored many aspects of life after addiction: emotional stability, building a strong mindset, handling worry, strengthening connections, planning for safety, transforming harmful thoughts, developing healthy activities, controlling urges, growing self-worth, communicating well, solving problems, finding balance, discovering meaning in uncertainty, managing anger, creating support networks, dealing with setbacks, and caring for your body and mind over time. Now it is time to gather all these threads and move forward with a sense of confidence and inner strength.

This chapter will focus on how to keep applying what you have learned in the long run. It will also explore ways to maintain progress when life changes or when you face new trials. Life after addiction is not a final destination; it is an evolving process of self-awareness, learning, and adapting. By combining your knowledge of healthy habits, emotional skills, and supportive resources, you can continue to grow in positive ways. The aim is to experience a steady sense of self-control and well-being that lasts—not perfection, but a stable, fulfilling path free from the old shadows of addiction.

20.1 Recognizing Your Progress So Far

Why It Matters
Looking back is not about getting stuck in the past; it is about seeing how far you have come. This can inspire you to keep going and remind you that you are capable of real change.

Ways to Acknowledge Growth

1. **Compare Old Habits to New**: Think about how you used to handle stress or sadness versus how you manage them today. Notice any improvements.
2. **Check Off Completed Goals**: If you wrote down aims or steps earlier, cross out what is done. Even small tasks count.

3. **Reflect on Emotional Changes**: Are you calmer or more patient with others? Do you recover from anger or sadness more quickly than before?
4. **Ask Close Supporters**: They might see changes you have overlooked, such as a more positive attitude or being more reliable.

By noticing these improvements, you reinforce the idea that continued progress is both real and possible.

20.2 Staying Vigilant Against Relapse

Why Vigilance Is Needed

Relapse can sneak up when you feel overconfident or forget to maintain your routines. Even if you have been free from harmful habits for a long time, stressful events or major shifts can weaken your defenses.

Ongoing Prevention

1. **Keep Key Routines**: Whether it is attending a weekly group, doing daily self-check-ins, or sticking to a particular stress management exercise, do not drop these habits just because you feel "fine."
2. **Watch for Warning Signs**: If you find yourself hiding negative emotions, lying to others, or reuniting with old crowds who engage in harmful behavior, these might be red flags.
3. **Plan for High-Risk Situations**: Holidays, big celebrations, or times of grief can be risky. Decide ahead of time how you will handle them—bring a supportive friend, limit your exposure, or keep a phone number handy to call if cravings appear.
4. **Refresh Your Toolbox**: Now and then, explore new methods to stay healthy, like an updated relaxation app, a different exercise routine, or a new mentor to talk to.

Treat vigilance not as fear, but as wise caution. You have worked hard to reach this point—protect that investment.

20.3 Continuing to Refine Emotional Skills

Just because you have learned anger management, stress control, or healthy communication does not mean the learning stops. Emotional skills can deepen over time.

Ideas for Ongoing Growth

1. **Take Advanced Workshops**: Many community centers or online platforms offer courses on conflict resolution, advanced communication techniques, or emotional intelligence.
2. **Regular Self-Reflection**: Weekly journaling or talking with a counselor can help you spot new emotional triggers or patterns.
3. **Experiment with Fresh Approaches**: If you have been using the same breathing technique for months, try a new relaxation method to keep your mind engaged.
4. **Teach Others**: Explaining emotional skills to friends or group members can reinforce your own mastery.

By continuing to fine-tune these skills, you ensure that you handle life's surprises with grace rather than panic.

20.4 Growing Your Social and Community Connections

Recovery is not a solitary experience. Maintaining strong ties with supportive people helps you stay motivated and cope with adversity.

Ways to Expand Connections

1. **Look for Local Interest Groups**: Clubs, volunteer organizations, or hobby meetups can lead to friendships with people who share healthy pursuits.
2. **Stay in Touch with Mentors**: If you have a sponsor or a counselor, keep them updated even when things are going well. Their advice can be helpful when new problems surface.
3. **Offer Support**: If you see others who are starting to break harmful habits, you might give them a listening ear or share your experiences. This can also remind you how far you have come.

4. **Family and Friends**: Continue to rebuild trust or strengthen bonds by organizing small gatherings, being there in times of need, and showing reliable behavior.

Community engagement fosters a sense of belonging and can protect you from slipping into isolation or old routines.

20.5 Protecting Your Lifestyle Changes During Life Shifts

Change is inevitable—new jobs, moving to different towns, changes in relationships, or shifts in financial status. These can disrupt your routines if you are not careful.

Strategies for Major Transitions

1. **Pack Your Best Habits**: If you relocate or change jobs, bring along the parts of your daily schedule that work well—like morning stretches or weekly recovery meetings (seek online options if needed).
2. **Scout Resources Early**: Before you relocate, research local therapists, clinics, support groups, or fitness centers that align with your plan.
3. **Stay Connected to Old Support**: Even if you move away, you can still call or video chat with mentors or friends who know your story. They can offer stability during uncertain times.
4. **Plan for Emotional Ups and Downs**: Transitions often come with stress or excitement that can trigger cravings. Keep using your self-care toolkit, and do not drop it just because life is changing.

By preparing for life's shifts, you avoid being knocked off balance whenever something big happens.

20.6 Balancing Confidence and Humility

Success in recovery can boost your self-esteem—a powerful thing after periods of struggle. However, it is essential not to become complacent or dismissive of potential pitfalls.

- **Stay Confident**: Acknowledge that you have gained knowledge, resilience, and coping skills. This self-belief is a positive force.
- **Stay Humble**: Accept that you are human, and relapse or setbacks can happen if you ignore warning signs. Keep your routines and remain watchful, even if you feel strong now.
- **Open Your Mind**: Be ready to learn from others, whether they have less or more time in recovery. Everyone's story can contain insights.

Confidence plus humility forms a healthy balance. You can trust in your progress while respecting the journey still ahead.

20.7 Setting New Goals Beyond Recovery

You have spent a lot of time focusing on quitting harmful habits and stabilizing your mental health. Over the long term, you might want to pursue goals that go beyond just staying clean or stable.

- **Career Growth**: Maybe you will seek a promotion, start a business, or retrain for a new field.
- **Education**: Explore courses, certifications, or workshops that spark your interest. It is never too late to learn something new.
- **Creative Outlets**: If you have an artistic side (drawing, music, writing), developing those skills can bring satisfaction and relieve stress.
- **Community Impact**: Some people find joy in volunteering, mentoring, or leading local initiatives—using their experiences to help others or improve their neighborhood.

Going beyond the basics of recovery can give you a sense of purpose and show that your life is not defined solely by the past addiction.

20.8 Maintaining Self-Kindness

After addiction, self-criticism can linger, especially if shame remains about past actions. Ongoing self-kindness ensures you do not revert to negative thinking patterns.

Practices for Self-Kindness

1. **Allow Normal Mistakes**: Humans mess up sometimes. When it happens, address it calmly, fix what you can, and move on without endless guilt.
2. **Positive Self-Reminders**: Remind yourself, "I am learning," or "I have faced difficult times and come this far."
3. **Healthy Self-Comfort**: If stress rises, do something soothing—like a warm bath, a relaxing walk, or a comforting meal—without the old, harmful escapes.
4. **Encourage Self-Care**: Keep your environment supportive—tidy spaces, uplifting reading, or a home setup that promotes calm.

This gentle approach wards off the inner critic that might try to sabotage your growth.

20.9 Being Prepared for Emotional Triggers

Even if you have handled urges and stress well, emotional triggers can appear unexpectedly. They might be memories of painful times, seeing an old friend who still uses, or even a random smell that brings back cravings.

- **Stay Grounded**: Use quick centering methods, like a few slow breaths or pressing your feet firmly into the ground.
- **Identify the Trigger**: Name it: "I am feeling anxious because I saw an old friend from my past using days."
- **Activate Your Support**: If the urge or feeling is strong, call someone, text a mentor, or use an online group immediately.
- **Create Quick Exits**: If you are in a place where triggers are overwhelming, have a plan to leave if you sense your control slipping.

Emotional triggers do not have to sink you. They are signals to use the skills you have accumulated.

20.10 Reviewing and Updating Your Support System

Your network of supporters, mentors, and role models may shift as you evolve. Some people might drift away, or you might meet new folks who align better with your current goals.

- **Stay Grateful for Past Support**: Even if your needs change, you can appreciate what others offered you at earlier stages.
- **Invite New Allies**: Seek out people who encourage your next steps, whether it is professional growth, spiritual exploration, or creative expression.
- **Strengthen Old Ties if Desired**: You might reconnect with family or friends you had distanced yourself from once you feel healthier. Proceed carefully, ensuring the relationship supports your new life.
- **Let Go of Toxic Connections**: If some ties are negative or push you back toward unsafe behaviors, it might be time to say goodbye or reduce contact.

A healthy, flexible support system grows along with you, offering fresh resources for each new stage of life.

20.11 Telling Your Story

You have a story—your experiences, lessons, and insights from dealing with addiction and rebuilding. Sharing that story, if and when you feel ready, can benefit you and others.

- **Confidence Builder**: Voicing what you have overcome can remind you of your own strength.
- **Inspiration for Others**: Someone new to recovery might find hope in hearing about your path.
- **Self-Awareness**: Telling your story forces you to organize events and feelings, which can shed light on your own growth.
- **Choose Safe Outlets**: You can share in a small support group, with a trusted friend, or perhaps in a written form if you prefer some distance.

Always respect your boundaries. You do not owe anyone your story, but it can be a powerful tool for community connection and self-affirmation if you choose to share it.

20.12 Celebrating Without Dangerous Behaviors

In earlier days, you might have associated parties, happiness, or success with drinking, using substances, or other risky behaviors. Now, you can discover new forms of positive recognition.

Healthier Ways to Mark Accomplishments

1. **Organize a Simple Gathering**: Invite a few close friends for a game night, potluck, or coffee chat. Keep the atmosphere relaxed and substance-free.
2. **Enjoy a Personal Treat**: Buy a small item you have wanted, take a nature trip, or indulge in a favorite meal that does not jeopardize your health.
3. **Reflect in a Meaningful Way**: Write down what you learned from a significant milestone, or make a short video diary to capture your feelings.
4. **Give Back**: Sometimes celebrating can involve helping someone else, like volunteering for a day in honor of your progress.

Replacing old celebrations with new, healthy ones cements the idea that joy and pride do not require returning to past harmful habits.

20.13 Handling Occasional Stumbles

Even far along in recovery, smaller missteps might happen. For instance, you might overwork yourself for a week, skip group meetings, or speak harshly to a loved one due to stress.

- **Own Up Quickly**: Acknowledge the stumble and decide to correct it. Pretending it is not happening can compound the problem.
- **Revisit Your Toolbox**: Use the methods from previous chapters—relaxation, problem-solving, communicating needs, or checking in with your support network.
- **Forgive Yourself**: A slip in habit or mood does not erase years of progress.
- **Learn**: Ask, "Why did this happen now?" and "How can I avoid a repeat?" Then adjust your routine or environment accordingly.

Minor stumbles are normal. Catching and correcting them promptly keeps them from escalating into full-blown crises.

20.14 Ongoing Self-Discovery

Recovery opens the door to self-discovery because you are no longer numbing pain or running away from uncomfortable truths. Over time, you can deepen your awareness of your personality, preferences, and purpose.

- **Explore New Interests**: Try a class or hobby you were always curious about. Your taste might surprise you.
- **Reflect on Inner Values**: You might refine your principles, perhaps focusing more on honesty, compassion, or community service.
- **Challenge Old Limits**: If you used to think you could never handle certain tasks or talk to certain people, test that limit now. You may find that your confidence has grown.
- **Stay Curious**: Approach each day with an openness to learning something about the world or about yourself.

This self-discovery can bring you a deeper sense of fulfillment and keep your life rich and stimulating.

20.15 Sustaining Motivation for the Long Term

Motivation will naturally ebb and flow. Sometimes you will feel on top of the world, and other times you may feel tired of routines. The key is to have systems in place to reignite your motivation.

- **Rotate Techniques**: If one habit or method becomes stale, switch it up. Instead of jogging, try cycling, dancing, or a new exercise class.
- **Celebrate Small Benchmarks**: Do not wait for giant successes. Every month, look at what has gone right, even if it is minor.
- **Look for Fresh Sources of Inspiration**: Read success stories, watch interviews, or attend talks by people who have overcome big challenges.
- **Remember the Cost of Quitting**: Think about what you risk losing if you abandon your healthy path. That can reaffirm your dedication.

Long-term motivation is about variety, reminders of why you chose this life, and the occasional spark from external inspirations.

20.16 Less-Known Approaches to Ongoing Strength

1. **Review Personal Milestones on a Calendar**: Circle dates of significant achievements—when you first quit, first tackled a big fear, or made an important apology. Glancing at these circles can boost your confidence.
2. **Set "Maintenance Weeks"**: Occasionally devote a week to reviewing all your routines—food, exercise, relationships, finances—to see if anything slipped. This is like a personal tune-up.
3. **Mentor Someone**: Taking on a mentee who is earlier in recovery can sharpen your own commitment. Teaching or guiding them often clarifies your own beliefs and skills.
4. **Creative Expression of Achievements**: Paint, write, or compose something that reflects your path. This can lock in your gains in a meaningful way, reminding you how far you have come.

These unique approaches can keep your momentum alive as you advance in your healthier lifestyle.

20.17 Overcoming the Myth of "Complete Repair"

One misconception is that there will be a day when you are "fully fixed" and never have to think about recovery again. In reality, many people live great lives while still staying mindful of their vulnerability to addictive behaviors.

- **Accepting Imperfection**: You do not have to be fully immune to urges or negative thoughts. What matters is your consistent response to them.
- **Daily Renewal**: Each morning can be a fresh start. You reaffirm your choice to stay well, even if yesterday was hard.
- **Strengthen What Works**: If you have found a routine that greatly reduces stress or cravings, stick to it. You do not have to fix what is not broken.
- **Evolve Without Pressure**: Some days might feel easy, others challenging. Embrace that flow, using the tools you have gathered.

Seeing recovery as a continuous path sets you free from the pressure of being "all done." Instead, you appreciate each day's progress as part of a lifetime of growth.

20.18 Key Points from Chapter 20

1. Acknowledging how far you have come can fuel your dedication to keep moving forward.
2. Vigilance is essential to prevent relapse, even after long periods of successful change.
3. Emotional skills can always be refined—learning never stops.
4. Healthy social connections evolve over time; remain open to new relationships and supportive communities.
5. Life changes like moving or shifting careers need careful planning to maintain your healthy routines.
6. Balancing confidence and humility keeps you grounded, recognizing your growth while staying mindful of potential pitfalls.
7. Going beyond basic recovery goals—pursuing career, educational, or creative ambitions—brings a deeper sense of purpose.
8. Self-kindness remains crucial, especially if a small slip or emotional setback happens.
9. Emotional triggers can appear any time. Keep your coping toolkit ready.
10. Updating your support system ensures you have people who truly fit your current needs and direction.
11. Sharing your story can reinforce your own progress and help others who are struggling.
12. Safe, substance-free forms of recognition or "celebration" help you enjoy achievements without risking relapse.
13. Minor stumbles do not undo all your hard work; address them quickly and learn from them.
14. Recovery opens doors to self-discovery—try new activities, challenge old fears, and refine your personal values.
15. Motivation for a healthier life can be sustained with variety, acknowledging small wins, and remembering your reasons for change.
16. Ongoing approaches—like a personal "maintenance week" or creative expression—keep your inner strength alive.
17. There may never be a complete "repair," but continuous growth is possible. You handle challenges each day with the wisdom you have gained.

Conclusion

Moving forward with inner strength means taking all the tools you have gathered—awareness of your emotional states, trust in yourself, effective communication, problem-solving abilities, healthy routines, support networks, and so on—and continuing to apply them in day-to-day life. It involves a balance between acknowledging your successes and staying open to learning more. Life will keep changing, but now you have a solid framework to handle the twists and turns without sinking back into old habits.

Recovery is not a straight line; it is an evolving process. With each new day, you have the chance to use these skills in fresh ways, build deeper relationships, and explore new goals. You can face disappointment and anxiety with healthy coping methods and lean on trusted allies for help. As time passes, the healthy habits you once had to force will often become second nature—an anchor that keeps you stable no matter what arises.

Above all, remember that you are not defined by your past or limited by old mistakes. You have learned how to protect yourself from harmful behaviors, nurture your mind and body, and step carefully into the future. The tools in this book are meant to be revisited whenever you need them—like a reference guide for continued growth. With consistent practice, ongoing support, and a steady focus on well-being, your life can flourish in ways that once seemed out of reach. This is your life beyond addiction: a safer, more meaningful existence shaped by courage, clarity, and the inner strength you have worked so hard to build.

www.ingramcontent.com/pod-product-compliance
Lightning Source LLC
LaVergne TN
LVHW012104070526
838202LV00056B/5611